Baby Names For Boys That Really Rock (2014)

Louise Nolan

Copyright 2014.

All rights reserved. No part of this book may be reproduced or transmitted in any form or by any means, electronic or mechanical, including photocopying, recording or by any information storage and retrieval system without written permission from the author.

Paperback and electronic versions published by:
Magnificent Milestones, Inc.

ISBN: 9781933819723

Disclaimer:

(1) This book was written as a guide; it does not claim to be the definitive word on baby names. Accordingly, the author and publisher do not accept any liability or responsibility for any loss or damage that have been caused, or allegedly caused, through the use of information in this book.

(2) To our knowledge, all of the information in this book is correct (and current) at the time of publication. However, trends can (and do) change on a daily basis, which will affect the popularity of any given name.

Table of Contents

Chapter 1: Introduction	4
Chapter 2: The Most Popular Baby Names for Boys	9
Chapter 3: A Blast from the Past - Top Names from the Past Decades	14
Chapter 4. Christian & Biblical Names	20
Chapter 5. Names from Literature & Mythology	23
Chapter 6. Names from Popular Culture / the Entertainment Industry	27
Chapter 7: Named after U.S. Presidents	33
Chapter 8. Names from Disney	35
Chapter 9. Names that are Ideals or Concepts	38
Chapter 10. Names from Nature	39
Chapter 11: Last Names as First Names	40
Chapter 12: Named After Famous Places	44
Chapter 13: One Syllable Names	46
Chapter 14: Lengthy (Four Syllable) Names	52
Chapter 15: Unisex / Gender Neutral Names	54
Chapter 16: Popular African-American Names	58
Chapter 17: Popular Hispanic Names	62
Chapter 18: Popular Asian Names	65
Chapter 19. Top 10 Names for Boys in Other Countries	68
Chapter 20: Names with Similar Meanings	70
Chapter 21. Names that Sound Alike	73
Appendix: An Alphabetical List of Names for Boys	75

Chapter 1. Introduction: The Challenges of Choosing the Perfect Name

Few things are more exciting - or complex - than choosing a child's name. The stakes are incredibly high: this beautiful little boy, who has no say in the matter, must live with *your* decision for the rest of his life. Even worse, you must make that decision before you know your son's personality and temperament, which determines whether or not the name you have chosen will truly "fit" him.

Years ago, when I perused various books of baby names, I was intrigued by the authors' arbitrary "rules" for first, middle, and last names. Yet, in reality, the beauty of a name is subjective - and what one person considers an excellent choice, another person may not. Thus, I offer only one hard and fast rule in this book: the only opinions that matter are those of the *parents* who will love and raise the baby boy they are naming. Other people may agree or disagree with your choice, but they don't have to live with it - and their input should be considered accordingly.

That being said, there are several factors to consider when choosing a name:

1. **Tradition / Femininity.** Do you want a masculine name or something that is gender neutral? Likewise, do you favor traditional boys' names or something modern or unisex? The difference:

| Zachary, Alexander, Jonathan | vs. | Blake, Brett, Flynn |
| Thomas, Brian, James | vs. | Quinn, Tai, Gus |

2. **The family's last name.** Ideally, the child's first, middle, and last names should have a pleasant flow. Ironically, what is "pleasing" to one family may seem harsh and abrupt to another.

For many parents, length and alliteration are also critical. Do you want your child to have a short name that is easy to write and spell - or do you believe that the beauty and flow of a longer name are worth the trade-off?

| Jonathan Alexander Jones | vs. | James Lee Jones |
| Maximilian Michael Miles | vs. | John Mark Miles |

3. **The uniqueness of the name.** Most parents follow trends, rather than start them. As a result, there are usually five or six students with the same name in every classroom, simply because it was popular the year they were born. In contrast, there will inevitably be one or two students in the same school who have unique names that no one has heard before.

Which of these scenarios do you prefer? Do you want your son to have a popular name that is easy to spell and pronounce, but not particularly creative? Or, do you favor distinctive names that will garner your child (possibly unwanted) attention? The difference:

| William Ryan White | vs. | Ziggy Stone White |
| Ethan Alexander Stanton | vs. | Rebel Legend Stanton |

Thankfully, there are thousands of names that fall between these two extremes that you can choose, depending upon your personal and familial preferences. When you consider your options, bear in mind: you are making this decision on behalf of a child whose personality may be very different from your own. Are you willing to take a risk - or would you prefer to play it safe?

4. **The longevity of the name**. That cute baby in your arms will eventually become a successful adult with dreams and aspirations of her own. Will the name you choose last a lifetime? In making this decision, consider the following questions - and whether the answers make a difference to you:

a. If given the choice between a physician named Rebel or John, which would you choose?

b. Likewise, can you imagine a district attorney - or circuit court judge - named Axl or Genesis?

The choice you make will affect how your child is perceived for his *entire life*. What seems "cute" now may not be nearly as desirable on a professional resume.

5. **Consider the initials** your child will have if you choose a particular name. If possible, avoid embarrassing combinations, such as IOU, LOL, PIG, FAG, and WTF. Many times, you can avoid bad combinations by choosing an alternative middle name.

6. If you choose a long or formal name, **consider the nickname** the child is likely to inherit. Some names, such as Alexander and Andrew, have multiple options, while others have only one. Even worse, once your child enrolls in school, you are unlikely to control whether or not an undesirable nickname "sticks." Bottom line: if you don't want your kids called Billy and Zack, don't name them William and Zachariah.

7. **Consider the spelling and pronunciation** of the name, which can be a source of confusion and frustration for many children. If you name your child Bartholomew or Xavier, there is an excellent chance that he will spend his entire lifetime explaining to people how to spell and pronounce it. This isn't "bad," per se, but it may be annoying for your child.

8. **Consider the meaning of the name**, if that is important to you. Unfortunately, some popular names have truly awful meanings:

Cameron means "crooked nose"
Kennedy means "ugly head"

Granted, most people do not know - or care about - the meaning of a given name. They simply take it at face value. But if the translation of a name (and the underlying connotation) bothers you, an alternative choice may be best.

9. **Pressures from relatives to choose a "family" name**. There is nothing inherently right or wrong with naming children after beloved relatives. In many cases, it is a lovely way to honor and preserve the memory of someone important to your family. Nevertheless, problems arise when:

a. the name is question is not particularly pleasing
b. the relatives pushing it will not take no for an answer

In these cases, middle names can be an excellent solution. In my experience, a child's middle name is usually chosen for one of three reasons:

a. it is a short, pleasant, and generic "placeholder" between the first and last names:

Examples: Stephen John Clark
                Alexander Lee Ruggerio

b. it is the "second choice" name that was vetoed at the last moment:

Examples: Elliott Ethan Miller
                  Alexander Jacob Ruggerio

c. it is the name of a beloved relative that the parents did not want to use as the first name:

Examples: Ethan Harold Miller
                  Alexander Clyde Ruggerio

Rather than argue with your sister, mother and spouse about a particular choice, using it as a middle name can be a great solution.

10. **Following - or avoiding - trends**. In recent years, there have been several trends in baby names that have influenced parents' choices, including:

- unisex (gender neutral) names
- last names as first names
- naming children after famous places
- creating unique names by adding/deleting letters and changing consonants or vowels
- using names from different cultures or eras
- naming children after celebrities, fictional characters, or historical figures

As a result, baby names are more varied and exotic than ever before. Nevertheless, some parents have resisted these trends in favor of classic and traditional names that will stand the test of time. This book, which presents more than 3,000 names for boys, offers extraordinary choices for *both* groups of parents- and for those who are still sitting on the fence. Use the lists as a starting point - and see what works best for you and your family. Experiment with different names that capture the sound and feel that you desire. Choose the name that perfectly reflects the baby boy you are carrying - and your hopes and dreams for his future.

How to Use this Book

By design, this book is arranged in a logical way:

1. the chapters are clearly labeled to guide your search

2. the names are presented in alphabetical order (unless noted otherwise)

3. the meaning of each name is clearly presented, although some names have multiple meanings, depending upon the original language and interpretation. Due to these variations, we encourage you to conduct additional research into the history and derivation of the names that you choose, both to learn more about them and to explore alternative spellings. By doing so, you can confirm that the name truly feels right and has no negative or unusual connotations.

4. in recent years, parents have expressed a preference for unisex, or gender neutral names that they can use for their babies, regardless of their sex. To honor this request - and to showcase the dozens of names that can be used for both boys and boys, this book presents an entire chapter of unisex names for you to consider.

5. finally, for readers who prefer a direct approach - or simply get tired or overwhelmed by the "themes" we have used, the final chapter of the book presents an alphabetical list of more than 3,000 names for baby boys.

Why 3,000, rather than the 100,000 presented in other books? Because we have streamlined the approach by focusing on the names that you are most likely to use, rather than including odd and esoteric choices from 200 years ago that no one can spell or pronounce. We have also avoided the temptation to turn Anthony into 20 different names, simply by making a few spelling changes.

And, that, ultimately, is the final topic of this chapter: the emerging trend of creating unique and customized names by varying the spelling of a classic name. In most cases, **that** is how most baby name books manage to present 50,000 choices - they include every possible alternative way to spell every name they present. On one hand, that is valid, because many parents like the idea of a unique name. On the other hand, it is somewhat misleading - is the name Aiden really all that different from Aydan? And do you really *want* to change the spelling of a classic name - knowing that your child will have to explain, correct, and re-spell it for the dozens of teachers, employers, and business contacts who get it wrong?

If the answer is yes, here is a quick summary of how to create a customized name.

1. **Change a consonant:**

C to K: Catherine/Katherine, Crystal/Krystal, Christine/Kristine
C to CH: Cris/Chris, Ciara/Chiara
C to S: Cheryl/Sheryl, Cynthia/Synthia
F to Ph: Filipe/Phillip, Felicia/Phylicia
G to J: Gillian/Jillian, Geoffrey/Jeffrey
X to J: Xavier/Javier
Z to S: Inez/Ines
H to S: Janesha/Janessa

2. **Change a vowel**:

A to E: Megan/Meagan
A to Y Megan/Megyn
CE to SS: Jocelyn/Josslyn
CI to SH: Lacrecia/Lacresha, Marcia/Marsha
E to Y: Karen/ Karyn, Hailee/Hailey
E to O: Conner/Connor, Ellery/Ellory
E to EI: Andre/Andrei, Keegan/Keigan
EO to E: Geoffrey/Jeffrey
I to Y: Nanci/ Nancy, Brandi/Brandy, Katherine/Kathryn
I to E: Austin/Austen
IE to Y: Debbie/Debby
O to EAU: Bo/Beau
U to EW: Drew/Dru
U to W: Laurence/Lawrence

3. **Add (or subtract) a letter or phrase:**

Add an O: Alphonso/Alphonse
Add an S: Apollo/Apollos
Add an E: Clancy/Clancey, Emil/Emile, Axl/Axel
Add an L: Alan/Allen, Chancellor/Chancelor
Add a "son:" Anders/Anderson
Add a "ton:" Fuller/Fullerton, Jack/Jackson
Add a "de:" Wayne/Dewayne
Add a "mac:" Kenzie/Mackenzie
Add a "lyn:" Brooke/Brooklyn, Joss/Josslyn

4. **Combine two names into one:**

Ashlyn: (American): a combination of Ashley and Lynn
Deandra: (American): a combination of Dee and Andrea
Deangelo: (Italian): a combination of De and Angelo
Kaylin: (American): a combination of Kay and Lynn

5. **Use non-traditional words as names**, such as places, surnames, and personal ideals (such as honor, heaven, and bliss). The chapters in this book will provide the inspiration you need to find distinctive and creative names from unusual and unlikely places. For more traditional parents, we have also included quality choices from history, literature, and the Bible. Use the lists as guidance and inspiration for your search - and choose the name for your baby that truly works best for you.

Chapter 2. The Most Popular Names for Boys

For many prospective parents, this chapter is a logical place to start - with the most popular names for boys in the United States. Ironically, readers like this chapter for two very different reasons: some love the idea of giving their child a popular and trendy name, while others hate the concept - and immediately dismiss all top names from consideration.

Regardless of your own inclination, it's fun to explore the current trends in names on a national basis, if only to know what other parents consider trendy and desirable. As you read and consider each name, you can use this information to add (or subtract) various possibilities from your list.

Finally, a word about "popular" names in a nation as large and diverse as the United States: different names are popular in different regions, depending upon the cultural, spiritual and socioeconomic backgrounds of their residents. In an area with many Asian families, for example, names such as Ling and Ming will be more popular than those in other communities. Likewise, in regions that are predominantly Christian, Biblical names will be more popular than those in communities that are spiritually diverse.

On a practical basis, this information may not affect you (or the choices that you make). But it *does* explain why the variation among children's names is so broad in different parts of the country. In some cities, there will be five Jasons in every classroom, but no one named Jose or Rashid. In other places, there will be several Javiers, but no one named or Ethan or John. Ultimately, the names in this chapter are the most popular in the US *on average*, which may (or may not) reflect the demographics in your own community.

Finally, a quick word about the source of this data, which is the U.S. Social Security Administration (SSA). Every child in the U.S. must have a Social Security number in order to be claimed on his/her parents' federal income tax forms (and to qualify for various benefit programs). Every year, the Social Security Administration records the popularity of names based on these applications and releases that information to the public. The SSA does not, however, break the data down by race or ethnicity - as a result, the rankings are averaged over all U.S. citizens who applied for a Social Security number in their child's name that year.

The names in this chapter are the most popular choices for baby boys who were born in the U.S. in 2012, which is the last year for which data is available. We have presented them in order of popularity, from 1 to 100.

1. Jacob: (Biblical): supplanter; (Hebrew): he grasps the heel

2. Mason: (French & English): stone worker

3. Ethan: (Hebrew & Biblical): firm, strong

4. Noah: (Biblical): rest, peace; (Hebrew): comfort, long-lived

5. William: (English, German & French): protector

6. Liam: (Irish & Gaelic): determined protector

7. Jayden: (American): God has heard

8. Michael: (Biblical & Hebrew): like God

9. Alexander: (Greek): protector of mankind

10. Aiden: (Irish, Celtic & Gaelic): fire, fiery

11. **Daniel:** (Hebrew & Biblical): God is my judge; (Irish & Welsh): attractive

12. **Matthew**: (Hebrew & Biblical): gift of the Lord

13. **Elijah:** (Biblical): the Lord is my God; (Hebrew): Jehovah is God

14. **James:** (English): supplant, replace; (Israel): supplanter

15. **Anthony:** (English & Biblical): worthy of praise

16. **Benjamin:** (English, Hebrew & Biblical): son of my right hand

17. **Joshua:** (Hebrew & Biblical): Jehovah saves

18. **Andrew:** (English, Scottish & Biblical): manly; brave

19. **David:** (Hebrew, Scottish & Welsh): beloved

20. **Joseph:** (Biblical): God will increase; (Hebrew): may Jehovah add/give

21. **Logan:** (Irish): small cove; (Scottish): Finnian's servant; (Gaelic): from the hollow

22. **Jackson:** (English): son of Jack; (Scottish): God has been gracious

23. **Christopher:** (Biblical): Christ-bearer; (English): he who holds Christ in his heart

24. **Gabriel:** (Israel): hero of God; (Hebrew): man of God; (Spanish): God is my strength

25. **Samuel:** (Israel): God hears; (Hebrew): name of God

26. **Ryan:** (Gaelic): little king; (Irish): kindly, young royalty

27. **Lucas:** (Gaelic, English & Latin America): light

28. **John:** (Israel): God is gracious; Jehovah has been gracious

29. **Nathan:** (Hebrew & Israel): gift of God

30. **Isaac:** (Biblical): he will laugh

31. **Dylan:** (English & Welsh): born from the ocean, son of the wave; (Gaelic): faithful

32. **Caleb:** (Hebrew): resembling an aggressive dog

33. **Christian:** (English & Irish): follower of Christ

34. **Landon**: (English): grassy plain; from the long hill

35. **Jonathan**: (Hebrew): Jehovah has given: (Israel): gift of God

36. **Carter:** (English): cart driver

37. **Luke**: (Greek & Latin America): light

38. **Owen**: (English, Welsh & Celtic); young warrior; (Irish): born to nobility

39. **Brayden:** (Irish & English): broad hillside; (Scottish): salmon

40. **Gavin:** (English): little hawk; (Welsh): hawk of the battle

41. **Wyatt:** (English): guide, wide, wood, famous bearer; (French): son of the forest guide

42. **Isaiah:** (Hebrew): the Lord is generous; (Israel): salvation by God

43. **Henry:** (English, German & French): rules his household

44. **Eli:** (Hebrew): ascended, uplifted, high; (Greek): defender of man

45. **Hunter:** (English): one who hunts

46. **Jack:** (English): God is gracious; (Hebrew): supplanter

47. **Evan:** (English): God is good; (Welsh): young; (Celtic): young fighter

48. **Jordan:** (Hebrew): to flow down; (Israel): descendant

49. **Nicholas:** (Greek): victorious people

50. **Tyler:** (English): maker of tiles

51. **Aaron:** (Jewish): enlightened; (Hebrew): lofty, exalted

52. **Jeremiah:** (Hebrew): may Jehovah exalt; (Israel): sent by God

53. **Julian/Julius/Julio:** (Spanish, French & Greek): youthful

54. **Cameron:** (Irish & Gaelic): crooked nose

55. **Levi/Levin:** (Hebrew & Israel): attached, united as one

56. **Brandon:** (Irish): little raven

57. **Angel:** (Spanish & Greek): angelic

58. **Austin:** (English): from the name Augustin, which means revered

59. **Connor**: (Irish): strong willed, much wanted

60. **Adrian:** (German, Spanish & Italian): dark; (Greek): rich

61. **Robert:** (English, French, German & Scottish): famed, bright, shining

62. **Charles:** (English): strong, manly

63. **Thomas:** (Hebrew, Greek & Dutch): twin

64. **Sebastian**: (Greek): the revered one

65. **Colton:** (English): coal town, from the dark town

66. **Jaxon**: (American): son of Jack

67. **Kevin:** (Irish & Gaelic): handsome, beautiful; (Celtic): gentle

68. **Zachary:** (Hebrew): Jehovah has remembered; (Israel): remembered by the Lord

69. **Aydan:** (Irish, Celtic & Gaelic): fire, fiery

70. **Dominic**: (Spanish): born on a Sunday

71. **Blake:** (English): pale, fair

72. **Jose**: (Spanish): God will add

73. **Oliver:** (French, English, Danish & Latin America): the olive tree; (German): elf army

74. **Justin:** (English & French): just, true; (Irish): judicious

75. **Bentley:** (English): from the bent grass meadow

76. **Jason:** (Greek): to heal

77. **Chase:** (English): hunter

78. **Ian:** (Scottish): gift from God

79. **Josiah:** (Hebrew): Jehovah has healed; (Israel): God has healed

80. **Parker:** (English): keeper of the park or forest

81. **Xavier**: (Spanish): owner of a new house

82. **Adam:** (Hebrew): red; (Israel): man of the earth; (English): of the red earth

83. **Cooper:** (English): barrel maker

84. **Nathaniel:** (Hebrew & Israel): gift of God

85. **Grayson:** (English): son of the bailiff

86. **Jace**: (American): God is my salvation

87. **Carson:** (English): son who lives in the swamp

88. **Nolan:** (Irish & Gaelic): famous; (Celtic): noble

89. **Tristan:** (English, Celtic & French): outcry, tumult; (Welsh): noisy; (Irish): bold

90. **Luis**: (Spanish): famous warrior

91. **Brody:** (Irish): brother, from the muddy place; (Scottish): second son

92. **Juan:** (Hebrew): gift from God; (Spanish): God is gracious

93. **Hudson:** (English): son of the hooded man

94. **Bryson**: (American): son of a nobleman

95. **Carlos**: (Spanish): a free man

96. **Easton:** (English): from east town

97. **Damian**: (Greek): one who tames others

98. **Alex:** (Greek): protector of mankind

99. **Kayden**: (American): fighter

100. **Ryder:** (English): knight

Chapter 3. The Evolution of Names Since 1900

While reading this book, you may wonder how (and why) names have evolved over time - and why some of your choices sound really strange to your parents and grandparents. In Chapter 2, we listed the most popular names for boys in the United States last year. In this chapter, we will take a look back at the same data at ten-year increments, beginning in 1900.

This exercise is fun for several reasons. First, it will allow you to see the types of names that were popular when your parents and grandparents were making the same decision that you are making today (when no one, and I mean, *no one*, named their baby Axel). Second, it reveals the names that are truly timeless - and those that only stayed popular for a few years. Third, it may spark your interest in names that you might otherwise not have considered, either for your son's first or middle name. You've just begun your search; before you consider a trendy name, it's worth looking back at some genuine classics, which were inspired by the leaders and celebrities of their time.

All data is from the official records of the U.S. Social Security Administration. For each year, names are presented in the order of popularity, from 1 to 20.

1900

1. **John:** (Israel): God is gracious; Jehovah has been gracious
2. **William:** (English, German & French): protector
3. **James:** (English): supplant, replace; (Israel): supplanter
4. **George:** (English): farmer
5. **Charles:** (English): strong, manly
6. **Robert:** (English, French, German & Scottish): famed, bright, shining
7. **Joseph:** (Biblical): God will increase; (Hebrew): may Jehovah add/give
8. **Frank**: (English): free man
9. **Edward:** (English): wealthy guardian; (German): strong as a boar
10. **Henry:** (English, German & French): rules his household
11. **Thomas:** (Hebrew, Greek & Dutch): twin
12. **Walter**: (German): the commander of the army
13. **Harry:** (German): home or house ruler
14. **Willie:** (English, German & French): a diminutive form of William, which means protector
15. **Arthur:** (English): bear, stone
16. **Albert:** (English & German): noble, bright
17. **Fred**: (German): peaceful ruler
18. **Clarence**: (English & Latin America): clear, luminous
19. **Paul:** (English & French): small, apostle in the Bible
20. **Harold**: (Scandinavian): ruler of the army

1910

1. **John:** (Israel): God is gracious; Jehovah has been gracious
2. **James:** (English): supplant, replace; (Israel): supplanter
3. **William:** (English, German & French): protector
4. **Robert:** (English, French, German & Scottish): famed, bright, shining
5. **George:** (English): farmer
6. **Joseph:** (Biblical): God will increase; (Hebrew): may Jehovah add/give
7. **Charles:** (English): strong, manly
8. **Frank**: (English): free man
9. **Edward:** (English): wealthy guardian; (German): strong as a boar
10. **Henry:** (English, German & French): rules his household
11. **Willie:** (English, German & French): a diminutive form of William, which means protector
12. **Thomas:** (Hebrew, Greek & Dutch): twin
13. **Walter**: (German): the commander of the army

14. **Albert**: (English & German): noble, bright
15. **Paul**: (English & French): small, apostle in the Bible
16. **Harry**: (German): home or house ruler
17. **Arthur**: (English): bear, stone
18. **Harold**: (Scandinavian): ruler of the army
19. **Raymond**: (German): wise protector
20. **Clarence**: (English & Latin America): clear, luminous

1920

1. **John:** (Israel): God is gracious; Jehovah has been gracious
2. **William:** (English, German & French): protector
3. **Robert:** (English, French, German & Scottish): famed, bright, shining
4. **James:** (English): supplant, replace; (Israel): supplanter
5. **Charles:** (English): strong, manly
6. **George:** (English): farmer
7. **Joseph:** (Biblical): God will increase; (Hebrew): may Jehovah add/give
8. **Edward:** (English): wealthy guardian; (German): strong as a boar
9. **Frank**: (English): free man
10. **Richard**: (English, French & German): a strong and powerful ruler
11. **Thomas:** (Hebrew, Greek & Dutch): twin
12. **Harold:** (Scandinavian): ruler of the army
13. **Walter:** (German): the commander of the army
14. **Paul:** (English & French): small, apostle in the Bible
15. **Raymond:** (German): wise protector
16. **Donald:** (Celtic & Gaelic): dark stranger; (Irish, English & Scottish): great leader
17. **Henry:** (English, German & French): rules his household
18. **Arthur:** (English): bear, stone
19. **Albert:** (English & German): noble, bright
20. **Jack:** (English): God is gracious; (Hebrew): supplanter

1930

1. **Robert:** (English, French, German & Scottish): famed, bright, shining
2. **James:** (English): supplant, replace; (Israel): supplanter
3. **John:** (Israel): God is gracious; Jehovah has been gracious
4. **William:** (English, German & French): protector
5. **Richard**: (English, French & German): a strong and powerful ruler
6. **Charles:** (English): strong, manly
7. **Donald:** (Celtic & Gaelic): dark stranger; (Irish, English & Scottish): great leader
8. **George:** (English): farmer
9. **Joseph:** (Biblical): God will increase; (Hebrew): may Jehovah add/give
10. **Edward:** (English): wealthy guardian; (German): strong as a boar
11. **Thomas:** (Hebrew, Greek & Dutch): twin
12. **Paul:** (English & French): small, apostle in the Bible
13. **Frank**: (English): free man
14. **Jack:** (English): God is gracious; (Hebrew): supplanter
15. **David:** (Hebrew, Scottish & Welsh): beloved
16. **Raymond**: (German): wise protector
17. **Kenneth:** (Celtic, Scottish & Irish): handsome; (English): royal obligation
18. **Harold:** (Scandinavian): ruler of the army
19. **Walter:** (German): the commander of the army
20. **Billy**: (English, German & French): a diminutive form of William, which means protector

1940

1. **James:** (English): supplant, replace; (Israel): supplanter
2. **Robert:** (English, French, German & Scottish): famed, bright, shining
3. **John:** (Israel): God is gracious; Jehovah has been gracious
4. **William:** (English, German & French): protector
5. **Richard:** (English, French & German): a strong and powerful ruler
6. **Charles:** (English): strong, manly
7. **David:** (Hebrew, Scottish & Welsh): beloved
8. **Thomas:** (Hebrew, Greek & Dutch): twin
9. **Donald:** (Celtic & Gaelic): dark stranger; (Irish, English & Scottish): great leader
10. **Ronald:** (English, Gaelic & Scottish): rules with counsel
11. **George:** (English): farmer
12. **Joseph:** (Biblical): God will increase; (Hebrew): may Jehovah add/give
13. **Larry:** (Dutch & Latin America): laurels
14. **Jerry**: (English): a diminutive form of Jerald, which means one who rules with the spear
15. **Kenneth**: (Celtic, Scottish & Irish): handsome; (English): royal obligation
16. **Edward:** (English): wealthy guardian; (German): strong as a boar
17. **Paul:** (English & French): small, apostle in the Bible
18. **Michael:** (Biblical & Hebrew): like God
19. **Gary:** (English): mighty spearman
20. **Frank**: (English): free man

1950

1. **James:** (English): supplant, replace; (Israel): supplanter
2. **Robert:** (English, French, German & Scottish): famed, bright, shining
3. **John:** (Israel): God is gracious; Jehovah has been gracious
4. **Michael:** (Biblical & Hebrew): like God
5. **William:** (English, German & French): protector
6. **David:** (Hebrew, Scottish & Welsh): beloved
7. **Richard:** (English, French & German): a strong and powerful ruler
8. **Thomas:** (Hebrew, Greek & Dutch): twin
9. **Charles:** (English): strong, manly
10. **Gary:** (English): mighty spearman
11. **Larry:** (Dutch & Latin America): laurels
12. **Ronald:** (English, Gaelic & Scottish): rules with counsel
13. **Joseph:** (Biblical): God will increase; (Hebrew): may Jehovah add/give
14. **Donald:** (Celtic & Gaelic): dark stranger; (Irish, English & Scottish): great leader
15. **Kenneth**: (Celtic, Scottish & Irish): handsome; (English): royal obligation
16. **Steven:** (English & Greek): crowned one
17. **Dennis:** (Greek): wild, frenzied
18. **Paul:** (English & French): small, apostle in the Bible
19. **Stephen**: (English & Greek): crowned one
20. **George:** (English): farmer

1960

1. **David:** (Hebrew, Scottish & Welsh): beloved
2. **Michael:** (Biblical & Hebrew): like God
3. **James:** (English): supplant, replace; (Israel): supplanter
4. **John:** (Israel): God is gracious; Jehovah has been gracious
5. **Robert:** (English, French, German & Scottish): famed, bright, shining
6. **Mark**: (Latin): dedicated to Mars, the god of war
7. **William:** (English, German & French): protector
8. **Richard**: (English, French & German): a strong and powerful ruler

9. **Thomas:** (Hebrew, Greek & Dutch): twin
10. **Steven:** (English & Greek): crowned one
11. **Timothy:** (Greek & English): to honor God
12. **Joseph:** (Biblical): God will increase; (Hebrew): may Jehovah add/give
13. **Charles:** (English): strong, manly
14. **Jeffrey:** (English): a man of peace
15. **Kevin:** (Irish & Gaelic): handsome, beautiful; (Celtic): gentle
16. **Kenneth:** (Celtic, Scottish & Irish): handsome; (English): royal obligation
17. **Daniel:** (Hebrew & Biblical): God is my judge; (Irish & Welsh): attractive
18. **Paul:** (English & French): small, apostle in the Bible
19. **Donald:** (Celtic & Gaelic): dark stranger; (Irish, English & Scottish): great leader
20. **Brian**: (Gaelic): noble birth; (Celtic): great strength

1970

1. **Michael:** (Biblical & Hebrew): like God
2. **James:** (English): supplant, replace; (Israel): supplanter
3. **David:** (Hebrew, Scottish & Welsh): beloved
4. **John:** (Israel): God is gracious; Jehovah has been gracious
5. **Robert:** (English, French, German & Scottish): famed, bright, shining
6. **Christopher:** (Biblical): Christ-bearer; (English): he who holds Christ in his heart
7. **William:** (English, German & French): protector
8. **Brian**: (Gaelic): noble birth; (Celtic): great strength
9. **Mark**: (Latin): dedicated to Mars, the god of war
10. **Richard**: (English, French & German): a strong and powerful ruler
11. **Jeffrey**: (English): a man of peace
12. **Scott**: (Scottish): wanderer
13. **Jason**: (Greek): to heal
14. **Kevin:** (Irish & Gaelic): handsome, beautiful; (Celtic): gentle
15. **Steven:** (English & Greek): crowned one
16. **Joseph:** (Biblical): God will increase; (Hebrew): may Jehovah add/give
17. **Thomas:** (Hebrew, Greek & Dutch): twin
18. **Eric:** (Scandinavian): honorable ruler
19. **Daniel:** (Hebrew & Biblical): God is my judge; (Irish & Welsh): attractive
20. **Timothy:** (Greek & English): to honor God

1980

1. **Michael:** (Biblical & Hebrew): like God
2. **Christopher:** (Biblical): Christ-bearer; (English): he who holds Christ in his heart
3. **Jason:** (Greek): to heal
4. **David:** (Hebrew, Scottish & Welsh): beloved
5. **James:** (English): supplant, replace; (Israel): supplanter
6. **Matthew**: (Hebrew & Biblical): gift of the Lord
7. **Joshua:** (Hebrew & Biblical): Jehovah saves
8. **John:** (Israel): God is gracious; Jehovah has been gracious
9. **Robert:** (English, French, German & Scottish): famed, bright, shining
10. **Joseph:** (Biblical): God will increase; (Hebrew): may Jehovah add/give
11. **Daniel:** (Hebrew & Biblical): God is my judge; (Irish & Welsh): attractive
12. **Brian**: (Gaelic): noble birth; (Celtic): great strength
13. **Justin:** (English & French): just, true; (Irish): judicious
14. **William:** (English, German & French): protector
15. **Ryan:** (Gaelic): little king; (Irish): kindly, young royalty
16. **Eric:** (Scandinavian): honorable ruler
17. **Nicholas:** (Greek): victorious people
18. **Jeremy:** (Israel): God will uplift

19. **Andrew:** (English, Scottish & Biblical): manly; brave
20. **Timothy:** (Greek & English): to honor God

1990

1. **Michael:** (Biblical & Hebrew): like God
2. **Christopher:** (Biblical): Christ-bearer; (English): he who holds Christ in his heart
3. **Matthew:** (Hebrew & Biblical): gift of the Lord
4. **Joshua:** (Hebrew & Biblical): Jehovah saves
5. **Daniel:** (Hebrew & Biblical): God is my judge; (Irish & Welsh): attractive
6. **David:** (Hebrew, Scottish & Welsh): beloved
7. **Andrew:** (English, Scottish & Biblical): manly; brave
8. **James:** (English): supplant, replace; (Israel): supplanter
9. **Justin:** (English & French): just, true; (Irish): judicious
10. **Joseph:** (Biblical): God will increase; (Hebrew): may Jehovah add/give
11. **Ryan:** (Gaelic): little king; (Irish): kindly, young royalty
12. **John:** (Israel): God is gracious; Jehovah has been gracious
13. **Robert:** (English, French, German & Scottish): famed, bright, shining
14. **Nicholas:** (Greek): victorious people
15. **Anthony:** (English & Biblical): worthy of praise
16. **William:** (English, German & French): protector
17. **Jonathan:** (Hebrew): Jehovah has given: (Israel): gift of God
18. **Kyle:** (Gaelic): young; (Irish): young at heart
19. **Brandon:** (Irish): little raven
20. **Jacob:** (Biblical): supplanter; (Hebrew): he grasps the heel

2000

1. **Jacob**: (Biblical): supplanter; (Hebrew): he grasps the heel
2. **Michael:** (Biblical & Hebrew): like God
3. **Matthew:** (Hebrew & Biblical): gift of the Lord
4. **Joshua:** (Hebrew & Biblical): Jehovah saves
5. **Christopher:** (Biblical): Christ-bearer; (English): he who holds Christ in his heart
6. **Nicholas:** (Greek): victorious people
7. **Andrew:** (English, Scottish & Biblical): manly; brave
8. **Joseph:** (Biblical): God will increase; (Hebrew): may Jehovah add/give
9. **Daniel:** (Hebrew & Biblical): God is my judge; (Irish & Welsh): attractive
10. **Tyler:** (English): maker of tiles
11. **William:** (English, German & French): protector
12. **Brandon:** (Irish): little raven
13. **Ryan:** (Gaelic): little king; (Irish): kindly, young royalty
14. **John:** (Israel): God is gracious; Jehovah has been gracious
15. **Zachary:** (Hebrew): Jehovah has remembered; (Israel): remembered by the Lord
16. **David:** (Hebrew, Scottish & Welsh): beloved
17. **Anthony:** (English & Biblical): worthy of praise
18. **James:** (English): supplant, replace; (Israel): supplanter
19. **Justin:** (English & French): just, true; (Irish): judicious
20. **Alexander:** (Greek): protector of mankind

2010

1. **Jacob**: (Biblical): supplanter; (Hebrew): he grasps the heel
2. **Ethan:** (Hebrew & Biblical): firm, strong
3. **Michael:** (Biblical & Hebrew): like God
4. **Jayden:** (American): God has heard
5. **William:** (English, German & French): protector

6. **Alexander:** (Greek): protector of mankind
7. **Noah:** (Biblical): rest, peace; (Hebrew): comfort, long-lived
8. **Daniel:** (Hebrew & Biblical): God is my judge; (Irish & Welsh): attractive
9. **Aiden:** (Irish, Celtic & Gaelic): fire, fiery
10. **Anthony:** (English & Biblical): worthy of praise
11. **Joshua:** (Hebrew & Biblical): Jehovah saves
12. **Mason:** (French & English): stone worker
13. **Christopher:** (Biblical): Christ-bearer; (English): he who holds Christ in his heart
14. **Andrew:** (English, Scottish & Biblical): manly; brave
15. **David:** (Hebrew, Scottish & Welsh): beloved
16. **Matthew**: (Hebrew & Biblical): gift of the Lord
17. **Logan:** (Irish): small cove; (Scottish): Finnian's servant; (Gaelic): from the hollow
18. **Elijah:** (Biblical): the Lord is my God; (Hebrew): Jehovah is God
19. **James:** (English): supplant, replace; (Israel): supplanter
20. **Joseph:** (Biblical): God will increase; (Hebrew): may Jehovah add/give

Chapter 4. Christian & Biblical Names for Twins

Across the U.S., Christian and Biblical names continue to be perennial favorites for both boys and girls. Depending upon your preference, you can follow this trend in a traditional or nonconventional way. Some names, such as Daniel and David, are extremely popular, while others, such as Demetrius and Zebulun, are relatively rare. Nevertheless, their place in history and religion gives them a strong global appeal. In this chapter, we present dozens of Christian and Biblical names in alphabetical order. Find the ones that suit your preference - and add them to your list.

Aaron: (Jewish): enlightened; (Hebrew): lofty, exalted
Abel: (Hebrew & Biblical): breathe, son

Abner: (Israel & Hebrew): father is light, father of light
Abraham: (Hebrew & Biblical): exalted father

Abram: (Hebrew): high father; (Israel): father of nations
Adam: (Hebrew): red; (Israel): man of the earth; (English): of the red earth

Alexander: (Greek): protector of mankind
Amos: (Hebrew): strong, carried, brave: (Israel): troubled

Andrew: (English, Scottish & Biblical): manly; brave
Anthony: (English & Biblical): worthy of praise

Apollos: (Israel): one who destroys
Asa: (Hebrew): physician; (Japanese): born at dawn

Asher: (Hebrew & Israel): happy, blessed
Azariah: (Hebrew & Israel): God helps

Barak: (Hebrew & Israel): flash of lightening
Barnabus: (Hebrew & Israel): comfort

Bartholomew: (English, Hebrew & Biblical): son of a farmer
Benjamin: (English, Hebrew & Biblical): son of my right hand

Cain: (Israel): craftsman; (Hebrew): spear; (Welsh): clear water; (Irish): archaic
Caleb: (Israel): faithful; (Hebrew): dog or bold

Christian: (English & Irish): follower of Christ
Christopher: (Biblical): Christ-bearer; (English): he who holds Christ in his heart

Claudius: (English): lame
Cornelius: (Irish): strong willed, wise; (Latin America): horn-colored

Daniel: (Hebrew & Biblical): God is my judge; (Irish & Welsh): attractive
David: (Hebrew, Scottish & Welsh): beloved

Demetrius: (Greek): goddess of fertility, one who loves the earth
Ebenezer: (Hebrew & Israel): rock of help

Eli: (Hebrew): ascended, uplifted, high; (Greek): defender of man
Elijah: (Biblical): the Lord is my God; (Hebrew): Jehovah is God

Emmanuel: (Hebrew): God with us
Ephraim: (Hebrew & Israel): fruitful

Esau: (Hebrew): hairy, famous bearer; (Israel): he that acts or finishes
Ethan: (Hebrew & Biblical): firm, strong

Evan: (English): God is good; (Welsh): young; (Celtic): young fighter
Ezekiel: (Hebrew & Israel): strength of God

Ezra: (Hebrew & Israel): helper
Gabriel: (Israel): hero of God; (Hebrew): man of God; (Spanish): God is my strength

Gideon: (Hebrew & Israel): great warrior
Ira: (Hebrew & Israel): watchful

Isaac: (Biblical): he will laugh
Isaiah: (Hebrew): the Lord is generous; (Israel): salvation by God

Ishmael: (Hebrew, Israel & Spanish): God listens, God will hear
Jacob: (Biblical): supplanter; (Hebrew): he grasps the heel

Jaden: (American): God has heard
James: (English); supplant, replace; (Israel): supplanter

Jeremiah: (Hebrew): may Jehovah exalt; (Israel): sent by God
Jeremy: (Israel): God will uplift

Jesse: (Hebrew): wealthy; (Israel): God exists; (English): Jehovah exists
Jethro: (Hebrew & Israel): excellence

Joab: (Israel): paternity, voluntary
Joel: (Hebrew): Jehovah is God; (Israel): God is willing

John: (Israel): God is gracious; Jehovah has been gracious
Jonah: (Hebrew & Israel): a dove

Jonathan: (Hebrew): Jehovah has given: (Israel): gift of God
Jordan: (Hebrew): to flow down; (Israel): descendant

Josiah: (Hebrew): Jehovah has healed; (Israel): God has healed
Joshua: (Hebrew & Biblical): Jehovah saves

Judas: (Hebrew & Israel): praised
Jude: (Israel): one who is praised

Justin: (English & French): just, true; (Irish): judicious
Justus: (Israel): fairness, justice

Lazarus: (Hebrew & Israel): God will help
Levi: (Hebrew & Israel): attached, united as one

Lucas: (Gaelic, English & Latin America): light
Luke: (Greek & Latin America): light

Marcus: (Gaelic): hammer; (Latin America): warlike
Mark: (Latin America): warlike

Matthew: (Hebrew & Biblical): gift of the Lord
Michael: (Biblical & Hebrew): like God

Micah: (Israel): like God
Moses: (Hebrew & Biblical): saved from the water

Nathan: (Hebrew): he gives; (Israel): gift of God
Nathaniel: (Hebrew & Israel): gift of God

Nicholas: (Greek): victorious people
Noah: (Biblical): rest, peace; (Hebrew): comfort, long-lived

Omar: (Arabian): ultimate devotee; (Hebrew): eloquent speaker
Paul: (English & French): small, apostle in the bible

Peter: (Greek & English): a small stone or rock, apostle in the bible
Philip: (French, Greek & English): lover of horses

Phineas: (Hebrew): oracle; (Israel): loudmouth
Reuben: (Hebrew & Israel): behold - a son

Rufus: (Latin America): redhead
Samson: (Hebrew & Israel): bright as the sun

Samuel: (Israel): God hears; (Hebrew): name of God
Saul: (Israel): borrowed; (Hebrew & Spanish): asked for

Sean: (Irish): God is gracious
Seth: (Hebrew): anointed; (Israel): appointed

Silas: (Latin America): man of the forest
Simon: (Israel): it is heard

Solomon: (Hebrew & Israel): peaceful
Stephen: (English & Greek): crowned one

Thaddeus: (Hebrew): valiant, wise: (Greek): praise, one who has courage
Thomas: (Hebrew, Greek & Dutch): twin

Timothy: (Greek & English): to honor God
Tobias: (Hebrew & Israel): God is good

Victor: (Spanish & Latin America): winner
Vincent: (English & Latin America): conquering, victorious

Zachary/Zachariah: (Hebrew): Jehovah has remembered; (Israel): remembered by the Lord
Zebulun: (Hebrew & Israel): habitation

Chapter 5. Names from Literature & Mythology

Many times, when you encounter a baby name that is mature, sophisticated, with a global appeal, it has its roots in literature and mythology. As expected, the popularity of these names has varied over time (and across geographical borders). Nevertheless, names from literature and mythology continue to hold a strong appeal for American parents who are passionate about history and the arts. In this chapter, we present a comprehensive list of names from literature and mythology in alphabetical order. See if your son's name is on the list!

Adonis: (Greek): beautiful
Ajax: (Greek): warrior

Ammon: (Egyptian): god of a unified Egypt
Amory: (German): ruler

Andre: (French): manly, brave
Angus: (Irish): vigorous one

Apollo: (Latin): strength, sun god
Ares: (Greek): god of war

Aristotle: (Greek): thinker with a great purpose
Arthur: (English): bear, stone

Atlas: (Greek): lifted, carried
Atticus: (Latin): a man from Athens

Balthazar: (English): the comedy of errors a merchant
Barrington: (English): town of Barr

Beau: (French): handsome, beautiful
Beowulf: (English): intelligent wolf

Burke: (German): birch tree
Carleton: (English): town of Charles

Casper: (Persian): treasurer; (German): imperial
Castor: (Greek): bereaved brother of Helen

Cato: (Latin): sagacious, wise one, good judgment
Chance: (English & French): good luck, keeper of records

Charles: (English): strong, manly
Clement: (French): compassionate

Cody: (Irish): helpful; (English): a cushion, helpful
Connor: (Irish): strong willed, much wanted

Cullen: (Irish & Gaelic): handsome; (Celtic): cub; (English): city in Germany
Damon: (English): calm, tame

Darcy: (Irish & Celtic): dark one
Dion: (French): mountain of Zeus

Dylan: (English & Welsh): born from the ocean, son of the wave; (Gaelic): faithful
Eamon: (Irish): blessed guardian

Ellison: (English): son of Elias
Faust: (Latin): fortunate

Finn: (English): blond
Fraser: (Scottish): strawberry flowers

Galen: (Gaelic): tranquil; (English): festive party: (Greek): healer, calm
Griffin: (Latin): prince, (Welsh): strong in faith

Hans: (German & Hebrew): gift from God; (Scandinavian): God is gracious
Heathcliff: (English): cliff near the heath

Hector: (Greek): anchor; (Spanish): tenacious
Henderson: (Scottish): son of Henry

Hermes: (Greek): stone pile
Hewitt: (English): little smart one

Holden: (English): from a hollow in the valley
Homer: (Greek & English): pledge, promise

Israel: (Israel): prince of God; (Hebrew): may God prevail
Janus: (Latin American): god of beginnings

Jarvis: (German): skilled with a spear
Jason: (Greek): to heal

Jasper: (Hebrew, French & English): precious stone
Johann: (German): God's gracious gift

Jonathan: (Hebrew): Jehovah has given; (Israel): gift of God
Jude: (Hebrew & Israel): praised

Jules: (French): youthful, downy-haired
Julian: (Spanish, French & Greek): youthful

Justin: (English & French): just, true; (Irish): judicious
Kana: (Japanese): powerful

Laird: (Scottish): lord; (Irish): head of household
Leander: (Greek): man of lions

Lewis: (German): famous warrior
Leo: (Italian & English): a lion

Loki: (Scandinavian): trickster god
Macon: (English): to make

Magnus: (Latin): great
Malloy: (Irish): noble chief

McKenna: (English): handsome, fiery
Merlin: (Welsh): of the sea fortress

Milo: (English): soldier
Oberon: (German): bear heart

Odin: (Scandinavian): ruler
Oliver: (French, English, Danish & Latin America): the olive tree; (German): elf army

Orion: (Greek): a hunter in Greek mythology
Orlando: (Spanish): land of gold: (German): famous throughout the land

Otto: (German): wealthy or prosperous
Pan: (Greek): god of flocks

Paris: (Persian): angelic face; (Greek): downfall; (French): the capital city of France
Philip: (French, Greek & English): lover of horses

Phineas: (Hebrew): oracle; (Israel): loudmouth
Pierre: (French): a rock

Plato: (Greek): strong shoulders
Pollux: (Latin American): brother of Helen

Puck: (English): elf
Quentin: (French, English & Latin America): fifth

Quillan: (Gaelic): resembling a cub
Raiden: (Japanese): god of thunder and lightning

Rhett: (English): stream
Ridley: (English): from the red meadow

Robin: (English): a diminutive form of Robert, which means famed, bright, shining
Romeo: (Italian, Spanish, Latin America & African American): from Rome

Rufus: (Latin America): redhead
Samson: (Hebrew & Israel): bright as the sun

Santiago: (Spanish): named for Saint James
Sawyer: (English): one who works with wood

Sebastian: (Greek): the revered one
Sheridan: (Irish, English & Celtic): untamed; (Gaelic): bright

Silas: (Latin America): man of the forest
Stern: (English): austere

Stuart: (Scottish): steward; (English): bailiff; (Irish): keeper of the estate
Taft: (French): from the homestead

Thor: (Norse): god of thunder
Tristan: (English, Celtic & French): outcry, tumult; (Welsh): noisy; (Irish): bold

Troy: (French): curly haired; (Irish): foot soldier
Tyr: (Norway): god of war

Ulysses: (Latin): hateful
Valentino: (Italian): brave or strong; (Latin America): health or love

Virgil: (English): flourishing; (Latin America): strong
Vulcan: (Latin): the god of fire

Wolf: (English): the animal, wolf
Yancy: (Native American): Englishman

Zeus: (Greek): powerful one

Chapter 6. Names from Popular Culture & the Entertainment Industry

Every year, parents seek new inspiration for their babies' names from the world of music, movies, sports, and television. As a result, the rise of a popular athlete, singer, or reality star can have a strong - and immediate - impact on a parent's choice of names. In some cases, such as Cyrus and Angus, the phenomenon brings new interest to classic names that had fallen out of favor. In other cases, such as Ashton and Ozzy, the phenomenon brings new names to the forefront that would otherwise not be considered.

My only caveat about names from popular culture is their shelf-life. Sixty years ago, millions of parents named their baby girls after Marilyn Monroe; however, its popularity waned within a few years. Nevertheless, some trends **do** manage to stick. After *Love Story* was released in 1970, millions of parents named their baby girls after the doomed heroine Jennifer ..... and the name continued to remain a top choice for more than 25 years.

When reviewing these names, try to be objective - and determine if you would still like the name if it was *not* associated with a famous person, character, movie, or song. Also consider the popularity of the name - and whether you want your child to be one of the seven Ashtons in his kindergarten class. In the end, there is no right or wrong answer - simply what feels right to **you**.

Ace: (Latin): unity
Adrian: (German, Spanish & Italian): dark

Aiken: (English): sturdy, made of oak
Anderson: (Scottish): son of Andrew

Angus: (Irish): vigorous one
Apollo: (Latin): strength, sun god

Ashton: (Hebrew): shining light; (English): ash tree settlement
Ari: (Hebrew): lion of God

Armand: (French): of the army
Armstrong: (English): strong arm

Arsenio: (Greek): masculine, virile
Austin/Austen: (English): from the name Augustin, which means revered

Avi: (Hebrew): my God, father; (Latin America): Lord of mine
Axl: (German & Hebrew): father of peace; (German): source of all life

Barak/Barack: (Hebrew & Israel): flash of lightening
Barrett: (English & German): strength of a bear

Beck: (English): the brook
Beckett: (English) : brook

Beckham: (Englidh): from the Beck homestead
Bjorn: (Scandinavian): a form of Bernard, which means strong as a bear

Bodhi: (Indian): awakens
Boone: (French): good

Boston: (English): the city Boston
Bowie: (Celtic): yellow-haired

Brady: (Gaelic & Irish): spirit; (Irish): broad-shouldered
Brandon: (Irish): little raven

Braxton: (English): from Brock's town
Brody: (Irish): brother, from the muddy place; (Scottish): second son

Bruno: (German): brown-haired
Bryce: (Scottish): speckled

Cameron: (Irish & Gaelic): crooked nose
Carlisle: (English): from the walled city

Carlton: (English): town of Charles
Casper: (Persian): treasurer; (German): imperial

Cassius: (Latin): empty, hollow, vain
Cato: (Latin): sagacious, wise one, good judgment

Cedric: (English): battle chieftain
Chandler: (French): candle maker

Chase: (English): hunter
Chauncey: (Latin): chancellor

Clay: (English): clay maker, immortal
Colbert: (French): famous and bright

Cole: (Irish): warrior
Conan: (English): resembling a wolf; (Gaelic): high and mighty

Cooper: (English): barrel maker
Cosmo: (Greek): the order of the universe

Creed: (English): belief, guiding principle
Crosby: (English): town crossing

Cullen: (Irish & Gaelic): handsome; (Celtic): cub; (English): city in Germany
Cyrus: (English): far-sighted

Damon: (English): calm, tame
Dane: (Hebrew & Scandinavian): God will judge; (English): brook

Darius: (Greek): kingly, wealthy; (American): pharaoh
Dax: (English & French): water

Dawayne: (Irish): dark
Deepak: (Hindu): little lamp

Denzel: (English): fort; African: wild
Dermot: (Irish): free from envy

Dexter: (Latin): right-handed, skillful; (Latin America): flexible
Dixon: (English): power, brave ruler

Dierks: (Danish): ruler of the people
Drake: (English): male duck, dragon,

Draper: (English): fabric maker
Dre: (American): a diminutive form of Andre, which means manly, brave

Drew: (English): courageous, valiant
Duncan: (Scottish): brown warrior

Dylan: (English & Welsh): born from the ocean, son of the wave
Edward: (English): blesses guardian

Eli: (Hebrew): ascended, uplifted, high; (Greek): defender of man
Elton: (English): old town

Elvis: (Scandinavian): wise
Emmett: (English): whole, universal

Evander: (Greek): benevolent ruler
Ewan: (Celtic, Scotch & Irish): young

Ezra: (Hebrew & Israel): helper
Finn: (English): blond

Fox: (English): fox
Frasier: (French): strawberry, curly-haired

Franco: (Italian): of France
Garth: (Scandinavian): keeper of the garden

Giovanni/Gian: (Italian); God is gracious
Godric: (English): power of God

Graham: (Scottish): from the gray home
Gray: (English): gray-haired

Grayson: (English): son of the bailiff
Gus: (German): revered

Guy: (French): guide; (Hebrew): valley; (Celtic): sensible; (Latin America): living spirit
Heath: (English): from the heath wasteland

Helio: (Greek): god of the sun
Hogan: (Irish & Gaelic): young, young at heart

Horatio: (French): hour, time
Hudson: (English): son of the hooded man

Hurley: (Irish): sea tide
Iggy: (Latin): fiery

Ioan: (Greek, Bulgarian & Romanian): a form of John, which means God is gracious
Jaden/Jayden: (American): God has heard

Jagger: (English): a carter, to carry
Jasper: (Persian): treasurer

Javier/Xavier: (Spanish): owner of a new house
Jay: (German): swift; (French): blue jay; (English): to rejoice; (Latin America): a crow

Jermaine: (French): a man from Germany; (Latin): brotherly
Jett: (English): resembling the black gemstone

Jonas: (Hebrew): gift from God; (Spanish): dove; (Israel): accomplishing
Juan Pablo: (Spanish): God is gracious/borrowed

Justin: (English & French): just, true; (Irish): judicious
Kareem: (Arabic): noble, distinguished

Keanu: (Hawaiian): of the mountain breeze
Keaton: (English): from the town of hawks

Kidd: (English): resembling a young goat
Kiefer: (German): one who makes barrels

Kieran: (Gaelic): the little dark one
Kingston: (English): from the king's village

Knox: (English): from the hills
Kobe/Kobi/Koby: (African): supplanter; (American): from California

Kramer: (German): shopkeeper
Laird: (Scottish): lord; (Irish): head of household

Lamar: (German): famous land; (French): of the sea
Leib: (Yiddish): roaring lion

Leif: (Scandinavian): beloved descendent
Levi/Levin: (Hebrew & Israel): attached, united as one

Levon: (Armenian): lion
Luc: (Latin): surrounded by light

Luka: (Latin America): light; (Russian): of Luciana
Maddox: (English): son of the Lord; (Celtic): beneficent

Magnus: (Latin): great
Marlon: (French): falcon, of the sea fortress

Marston: (English): from the town near the marsh
Mason: (French & English): stone worker

Maximus: (Greek): greatest
Miller: (English): one who works at the mill

Milo: (English): soldier
Montel: (Italian): mountain

Moroccan: (African): one from Morocco
Nash: (American): adventurer

Naveen: (Hindu): new; (Irish): beautiful, pleasant
Neo: (Greek & American): new

Niles: (English): champion
Orlando: (Spanish): land of gold: (German): famous throughout the land

Oz: (Hebrew): having great strength
Ozzy: (English): divine ruler

Quincy: (English): fifth; (French): estate belonging to Quintus
Quinn: (Celtic): wise; (Irish): fifth, counsel, intelligent

Pax: (English): peaceful
Penn: (Latin): pen, quill

Percy: (English): piercing the valley
Perry: (English): a familiar form of Peter, which means a small stone or rock

Peyton: (English): from the village of warriors
Peeta: (Indian): yellow silk cloth

Pharell/Pharrell: (American): of proven courage
Phineas: (Hebrew): oracle; (Israel): loudmouth

Presley: (English): priest's land
Radcliff: (English): red cliff

Rain/Raine: (American): blessings from above; (French & Latin): ruler; (English): lord, wise
Regis: (Latin): regal; (Latin America): rules

Reilly: (Gaelic): outgoing
Rio: (Portuguese): river

Ripley: (English): from the noisy meadow
River: (English): from the river

Rupert: (German): bright fame
Robin: (English): a diminutive form of Robert, which means famed, bright, shining

Rocco: (Italian & German): rest
Rocket: (English): fast

Roman: (Spanish & Latin America): from Rome
Ryder: (English): knight

Sanjay: (American): a combination of Sanford and Jay
Satchel: (French): Saturn

Sawyer: (English): one who works with wood
Sayid: (African): lord and master

Shane: (Hebrew): gift from God; (Irish): God is gracious
Shepherd: (English): one who herds sheep

Seven: (American): the number seven
Silas: (Latin America): man of the forest

Slater: (English): one who works with slate
Speck: (German): bacon

Spencer: (English): provider
Stanford: (English): from the stony ford

Sully: (English): from the southern meadow
Taye: (Ethiopian): *one who has been seen*

Terence: (Latin America): tender, gracious
Terrell: (German): thunder ruler

Tex: (English): of Texas
Tiger: (English): powerful cat

Trey: (English & Latin): third-born child
Trigg: (Norse): truthful

Tripp: (English): traveler
Troy: (French): curly haired; (Irish): foot soldier

True: (English): loyal
Tucker: (English): tucker of cloth

Tyrell: (American & English): thunder ruler
Tyson: (French): explosive; (English): son of Tye

Upton: (English): upper town
Urban: (Latin): city dweller, courteous

Usher: (Latin): from the mouth of the river; (English): doorkeeper
Vaughn: (Celtic): small

Wentworth: (English): village, from the white one's estate
Wesley: (English): from the west meadow

West: (English): from the west
Weston: (English): west town

Ziggy: (Latvian & Russian): a form of Siegfried, which means victorious peace

Chapter 7. Named After U.S. Presidents

The names of U.S. Presidents and First Ladies are favorites for many prospective parents. This is particularly true in election years, when the country "meets" the candidates' spouses and families for the first time. In this chapter, we will explore the names of U.S. Presidents that have stood the test of time; they also provide a fascinating glimpse into the distinguished men who have lived in the White House and governed our nation during the past two centuries

Abraham: (Hebrew & Biblical): exalted father
Andrew: (English, Scottish & Biblical): manly; brave

Arthur: (English): bear, stone
Barack: (Hebrew & Israel): flash of lightening

Benjamin: (English, Hebrew & Biblical): son of my right hand
Calvin: (English & Latin America): bald

Carter: (English): cart driver
Chester: (English): a rock fortress

Clinton: (English): town on a hill
Dwight: (English): a diminutive form of DeWitt, which means blond hair

Ford: (English): from the river crossing
Franklin: (English): free man

Garfield: (English): battlefield
George: (English): farmer

Gerald: (German): one who rules with the spear
Grant: (Latin): great

Grover: (English): grove
Harding: (English): brave, manly

Harrison: (English): son of Harry
Harry: (German): home or house ruler

Hayes: (English): from the hedged place
Herbert: (German): glorious soldier

Howard: (English): guardian of the home
Jackson: (English): son of Jack; (Scottish): God has been gracious

James: (English): supplant, replace; (Israel): supplanter
Jefferson: (English): son of Jeffrey, which means divine peace

John: (Israel): God is gracious; Jehovah has been gracious
Johnson: (Scottish & English): son of John

Kennedy: (Scottish): ugly head; (Irish & Gaelic): helmeted
Lincoln: (English): Roman colony at the pool; (Latin America): village

Lyndon: (English): flexible
Madison: (English): son of Matthew

Martin: (Latin): dedicated to Mars, the god of war
McKinley: (English): offspring of the fair hero

Monroe: (Gaelic): from the red swamp; (Scottish): from the river; (Irish): near the river roe
Nixon: (English): son of Nick

Quincy: (English): fifth; (French): estate belonging to Quintus
Pierce: (English): rock

Reagan: (Celtic): regal; (Irish): son of the small ruler
Richard: (English, French & German): a strong and powerful ruler

Ronald: (English, Gaelic & Scottish): rules with counsel
Roosevelt: (Danish): from the field of roses

Rutherford: (English): from the cattle's ford
Taft: (French): from the homestead

Taylor: (English & French): a tailor
Theodore: (Greek): divine gift

Thomas: (Hebrew, Greek & Dutch): twin
Truman: (English): loyal, trusted man; (German): faithful man

Tyler: (English): maker of tiles
Ulysses: (Latin): hateful

Warren: (English): to preserve; (German): protector, loyal
Washington: (English): town near water

William: (English, German & French): protector
Wilson: (English & German): son of William

Woodrow: (English): forester, row of houses
Zachary: (Hebrew & Israel): remembered by God

Chapter 8. Names from Disney

In reality, this material could easily be included in Chapter 6, which presents baby names from popular culture and the entertainment industry. But, on a practical basis, Disney has a greater reach - and longer staying power - than most musical, athletic, and movie franchises, which is why we have given it a chapter all its own.

Within a few months of a Disney release, the names of its characters begin to ascend the list of popular baby names. As a result, they bring the same benefits and pitfalls of other trendy names: everyone knows why you chose it..... and they probably chose it, too!

In the past few years, here are the most popular boys' names from Disney movies (in alphabetical order). See if one of them is right for *your* little prince.

Abu: (African): father
Aladdin: (Arabian): faithful

Andrew/Andy: (English, Scottish & Biblical): manly; brave
Apollo: (Latin): strength, sun god

Archimedes: (Greek): to think about first
Arthur: (English): bear, stone

Ben: (English): son of my right hand
Bruce: (French & English): woods, thick brush

Chip: (English): chipping sparrow
Christopher: (Biblical): Christ-bearer; (English): he who holds Christ in his heart

Clayton: (English): mortal
Dale: (German): valley; (English): lives in the valley

Dashiell: (French): page boy
David: (Hebrew, Scottish & Welsh): beloved

Donald: (Celtic & Gaelic): dark stranger; (Irish, English & Scottish): great leader
Doug: (Scottish): dark river

Eli: (Hebrew): ascended, uplifted, high; (Greek): defender of man
Fagin: (Gaelic): ardent; (Irish): eager

Fenton: (English): from the farm on the fens
Finn: (English): blond

Flynn: (Irish): heir to the red-headed
Gaetan: (French & Italian): from Italy

Gaston: (French): a man from Gastony
Gideon: (Hebrew & Israel): great warrior

Gus: (German): revered
Hercules: (Greek): son of Zeus

Hermes: (Greek): stone pile
Horace: (French): hour, time

Iago: (Welsh): Spanish supplanter
Ian: (Scottish): gift from God

Jack: (English): God is gracious; (Hebrew): supplanter
Jafar: (Hindu): little stream

Jake: (Hebrew): he grasps the heel
Jasper: (Persian): treasurer

Jock: (Scottish): God is gracious
Ken: (Welsh): clear water; (English): royal obligation; (Irish): handsome; (Japanese): strong

Kevin: (Irish & Gaelic): handsome, beautiful; (Celtic): gentle
Lafayette: (Israel): to God to the mighty

Lawrence: (Latin America): crowned with laurel
Louis: (French): famous warrior

Lucifer: (Israel): bringing light
Lyle: (French & English): from the island

Maurice: (Latin): dark-skinned
Maximus: (Greek): greatest

Mickey: (Irish, English & Hebrew): diminutive of Michael, which means like God
Milo: (English): soldier

Nemo: (Greek): glen, glade
Oliver: (French, English, Danish & Latin America): the olive tree; (German): elf army

Orville: (French): golden city; (English): spear-strength
Oswald: (English): the power of God

Otto: (German): wealthy or prosperous
Pascal: (French): born at Easter

Pegasus: (Greek): winged horse
Percy: (English): piercing the valley

Peter: (Greek & English): a small stone or rock, apostle in the Bible
Philip: (French, Greek & English): lover of horses

Preston: (English): from the priest's farm
Randall: (German): the wolf shield

Remy: (French): oarsman or rower, from Rheims
Rex: (Latin): king

Robin: (English): a small bird
Roscoe: (Norwegian): deer forest

Rufus: (Latin America): redhead
Russell: (French): a little red-haired boy

Sebastian: (Greek): the revered one
Sid/Sidney: (English): wide island

Simba: (African): lion
Terrence: (Latin America): tender, gracious

Timon: (Hebrew): honor
Timothy: (Greek & English): to honor God

Tito: (Italian): honor
Winston: (English): joy stone

Woodey: (English): wooded meadow
Zeus: (Greek): powerful

Chapter 9. Names that are Ideals or Concepts

A fascinating trend is the use of personal ideals - such as Justice and Unity - as baby names. These noble concepts are valued in all cultures, which gives the names a global appeal. Additionally, most of them are relatively rare, which increases their cachet. In this chapter, we present a list of ideal or concept names for baby boys in alphabetical order. Perhaps one of them will be right for your little angel.

Creed: (English): belief, guiding principle
Earnest: (English): industrious

Ernest: (German): serious, determined, truth
Freeborn: (English): child of freedom

Freeman: (English): free
Goode: (English): upstanding

Hero: (Greek): great defender
Journey: (American): one who likes to travel

Justice/Justus: (English): fair and moral
Legend: (American): memorable

Loyal: (English): faithful, loyal
Rebel: (American): outlaw

Unique: (Latin): only one; (American): unlike others
Unity: (English): unity, togetherness

Young: (Korean): forever, unchanging

Chapter 10. Names from Nature

People differ greatly in their temperament and ideals. Many times, our only commonality is the planet we inhabit - and the beautiful flowers, oceans, foods, colors, and gemstones that we all enjoy. As a result, names from nature are perennial favorites for boys in all cultures. In this chapter, we present an intriguing collection of boys' names that honor the incomparable beauty of nature.

Basil: (Greek & Latin): royal, kingly
Bay: (Vietnamese): born on a Saturday; (American): a natural body of water

Birch: (English): white, shining
Brock: (English): badger

Clay: (English): clay maker, immortal
Cliff: (English): from the ford near the cliff

Colt: (American): baby horse; (English): from the dark town
Drake: (English): male duck, dragon

Eagle: (Native American): resembling the bird
Finch: (Irish): resembling the small bird

Flint: (English): stream, hard quartz rock
Forrest: (English & French): from the woods

Fox: (English): fox
Glade: (English): from the clearing in the woods

Glenn: (Scottish): glen, valley
Hawk: (English): hawk

Hawkins: (English): resembling a small hawk
Heath: (English): from the heath wasteland

Hunter: (English): one who hunts
Hyde: (English): animal hide

Jett: (English): resembling the black gemstone
Leif: (Scandinavian): beloved descendent

Raine: (American): blessings from above; (Latin): ruler; (English): lord, wise
Ridge: (English): from the ridge

River: (English): from the river
Robin: (English): a small bird

Sage: (English & French): wise one; (English): from the spice
Sailor: (American): sailor

Silver: (English): precious metal, the color silver
Storm: (English): tempest; (American): impetuous nature

Thorne: (English): from the thorn bush
Wolf: (English): the animal, wolf

Chapter 11. Last Names as First Names

In the past decade, one of the most popular trends is the use of last names as first names for both boys and girls This approach offers parents a creative way to honor a cherished surname or to give their child a gender neutral (unisex) moniker that will be easy to remember. Alternatively, these choices also make excellent middle names.

In this chapter, we have included the most popular pairs of last names as first names (in alphabetical order). Use the list to narrow your search - or as inspiration for your own unique choices.

Abbott: (Hebrew): father
Alton: (English): from the old town

Ames: (French): friend
Ashton: (Hebrew): shining light; (English): ash tree settlement

Avery: (English): counselor, sage, wise
August: (German): revered

Addison: (English): son of Adam
Anderson: (Scottish): son of Andrew

Bailey: (English): bailiff, steward, public official
Brown: (English): brown color, dark-skinned

Bellamy: (French): handsome
Bowen: (Gaelic): small son; (Irish): archer

Black: (English): dark-skinned
Blake: (English): pale, fair

Brooks: (English): running water, son of Brooke
Brogan: (Gaelic & Irish): from the ditch

Brady: (Irish): a large-breasted woman
Blair: (Irish & Celtic): from the plain, (Gaelic): child of the fields; (Scottish): peat moss

Campbell: (Gaelic): crooked mouth; (French): from the beautiful field
Cullen: (Irish & Gaelic): handsome; (Celtic): cub; (English): city in Germany

Chase: (English): hunter
Curran: (Celtic): hero

Casey: (Celtic & Gaelic): brave; (Irish): observant, alert, brave; (Spanish): honorable
Cameron: (Irish & Gaelic): crooked nose

Carson: (English): son who lives in the swamp
Cain: (Israel): craftsman; (Hebrew): spear; (Welsh): clear water; (Irish): archaic

Carter: (English): cart driver
Chen: (Chinese): great, dawn

Cramer: (English): full
Crosby: (English): town crossing

Drew: (English): courageous, valiant
Davis: (English & Scottish): David's son

Drake: (English): male duck, dragon
Dixon: (English): power, brave ruler

Emerson: (English): brave, powerful
Elliott: (Israel): close to God; (English): the Lord is my God

Easton: (English): from east town
Ennis: (Irish): island; (Gaelic): the only choice

Ford: (English): river crossing
Franklin: (English): free man

Foster: (English & French): one who keeps the forest
Gallagher: (Irish & Gaelic): eagle helper

Fletcher: (English): one who makes arrows
Fleming: (English): from Denmark

Fitzgerald: (English): the son of Gerald
Fitzpatrick: (English): son of Patrick

Flynn: (Irish): ruddy complexion
Ford: (English): from the river crossing

Grant: (Latin): great
Gannon: (Irish & Gaelic): fair-skinned

Grayson: (English): son of the bailiff
Graham: (Scottish): from the gray home

Haines: (English): from the vine-covered cottage
Hayden: (English & Welsh): in the meadow or valley

Hilton: (English): town on a hill
Henderson: (Scottish): son of Henry

Hunter: (English): one who hunts
Holt: (English): wood, by the forest

Hogan: (Irish & Gaelic): young, young at heart
Howard: (English): guardian of the home

Jordan: (Hebrew): to flow down; (Israel): descendant
Jensen: (Scandinavian): God is gracious

Jackson: (English): son of Jack; (Scottish): God has been gracious
Johnson: (Scottish & English): son of John

Jagger: (English): a carter, to carry
Jefferson: (English): son of Jeffrey, which means divine peace

Kane: (Welsh): beautiful; (Gaelic): little warrior
Keaton: (English): from the town of hawks

Kendall: (English & Celtic): from the bright valley
Kennedy: (Scottish): ugly head; (Irish & Gaelic): helmeted

Kirkland: (English): from the church's land
Kramer: (German): shopkeeper

Landon: (English): grassy plain; from the long hill
Lawrence: (Latin America): crowned with laurel

Lincoln: (English): Roman colony at the pool; (Latin America): village
Logan: (Irish): small cove; (Scottish): Finnian's servant; (Gaelic): from the hollow

London: (English): fortress of the moon
Lewis: (German): famous warrior

Mackenzie: (Irish & Scottish): fair, favored one
Meyer: (Jewish & Hebrew): shining

Morgan: (Celtic): lives by the sea; (Welsh): bright sea
Marlowe: (English): from the hill by the lake

Macdonald: (Scottish): son of Donald
Malloy: (Irish): noble chief

Madison: (English): son of Matthew
Monroe: (Gaelic): from the red swamp; (Scottish & Irish): near the river roe

Marshall: (French): caretaker of horses; (English): a steward
Martin: (Latin): dedicated to Mars, the god of war

Miller: (English): one who works at the mill
Maxwell: (English): capable, great spring

Nash: (American): adventurer
North: (English): from the north

Moore & Murphy

Moore: (French): dark-skinned; (Irish & French): surname
Murphy: (Gaelic): warrior of the sea

Nolan: (Irish & Gaelic): famous; (Celtic): noble
Nelson: (English, Celtic, Irish & Gaelic): son of Neil

Nash: (American): adventurer
Newman: (English): a newcomer

Oliver: (French, English, Danish & Latin America): the olive tree; (German): elf army
Osborne: (Norse): a bear of God

Payton: (English): village
Paxton: (English): from the peaceful farm; (Latin America): town of peace

Parker: (English): keeper of the park or forest
Porter: (French): gate keeper; (Latin America): door guard

Reagan: (Celtic): regal; (Irish): son of the small ruler
Riley: (Irish): a small stream

Ryan: (Gaelic): little king; (Irish): kindly, young royalty
Rowan: (Irish): red-haired; (English & Gaelic): from the rowan tree

Reese: (Welsh): enthusiastic
Rylan: (English); dweller in the rye field

Quinn: (Celtic): wise; (Irish): fifth, counsel, intelligent
Quentin: (French, English & Latin America): fifth

Shea: (Irish): majestic, fairy place
Smith: (English): artisan, tradesman

Scully: (Irish): herald; (Gaelic): town crier
Silver: (English): the color silver

Sawyer: (English): one who works with wood
Sheldon: (English): from the steep valley

Tanner: (English & German): leather worker
Terrell: (German): thunder ruler

Tate: (English): cheerful
Tyler: (English): maker of tiles

Taylor: (English & French): a tailor
Thomas: (Hebrew, Greek & Dutch): twin

West: (English): from the west
Winter: (American): the season

Wyatt: (English): guide, wide, wood, famous bearer; (French): son of the forest guide
Wilson: (English & German): son of William

Chapter 12. Named After Famous Places

This chapter explores a fascinating trend that has emerged in the past two decades: the use of city, state, and country names for both boys and girls. Some of these choices are fairly common, such as Austin and Camden, while others are esoteric, such as Flint and Fullerton. Nevertheless, the trend is real, the names are eclectic, and the variety can't be beat. So, sit back and explore the most popular boys' names (in alphabetical order) that are based on famous places.

Austin: (English): from the name Augustin, which means revered
Ames: (French): friend

Alton: (English): from the old town
Aiken: (English): sturdy, made of oak

Boston: (English): the city Boston
Beaumont: (French): beautiful mountain

Berkeley: (English & Irish): from the birch meadow
Benson: (English): son of Benedict

Bentley: (English): from the bent grass meadow
Barrington: (English): town of Barr

Chester: (English): a rock fortress
Clayton: (English): mortal

Camden: (Irish, Scottish, English & Gaelic): from the winding valley
Carlin: (Irish, Gaelic & Scottish): little champion

Clyde: (Irish): warm
Carlisle: (English): from the walled city

Cody: (Irish): helpful; (English): a cushion, helpful
Chandler: (French): candle maker

Colton: (English): coal town, from the dark town
Columbus: (Greek): curious

Derby: (English): deer park; (Irish): from the village of dames
Devon: (English & Irish): a poet, a county in England

Diego: (Spanish): Saint James
Dallas: (Irish & Gaelic): wise; (Scottish & Celtic): from the waterfall

Easton: (English): from east town
Everett: (English): hardy, brave, strong

Fairbanks: (English): from the bank along the path
Fargo: (American): jaunty

Frederick: (German): peaceful ruler
Flint: (English): stream, hard quartz rock

Fremont: (French): protector of freedom
Fuller/Fullerton: (English): from Fuller's town

Jordan: (Hebrew): to flow down; (Israel): descendant
Jackson: (English): son of Jack; (Scottish): God has been gracious

Hartley: (English): from the stage meadow
Hadley: (English & Irish): from the heath covered meadow

Holland: (American): from the Netherlands
Houston: (Gaelic): from Hugh's town: (English): from the town on the hill

Kent: (English & Welsh): white; (Celtic): chief
Kingston: (English): from the king's village

Lincoln: (English): Roman colony at the pool; (Latin America): village
Lawrence: (Latin America): crowned with laurel

Logan: (Irish): small cove; (Scottish): Finnian's servant; (Gaelic): from the hollow
Landon: (English): grassy plain, from the long hill

London: (English): fortress of the moon
Livingston: (English): Leif's town

Mitchell: (Hebrew): gift from God
Maxwell: (English): capable, great spring

Mason: (French & English): stone worker
Merrill: (English): falcon, shining sea

Orlando: (Spanish): land of gold
Oliver: (French, English, Danish & Latin America): the olive tree; (German): elf army

Ramsey: (Scottish): island of ravens
Redford: (English): over the red river, from the reedy ford

Raleigh: (English): deer meadow
Radcliff/Radcliffe: (English): red cliff

Salem: (Hebrew): peace
Salisbury: (English): fort at the willow pool

Trenton: (English): town of Trent
Tanner: (English & German): leather worker

Texas: (Native American): one of many friends, from the state of Texas
Tennessee: (Native American): from the state of Tennessee

York: (Celtic, English & Latin America): from the yew tree
Vernon: (Latin): youthful, young at heart; (French & English): alder tree grove

Warren: (English): to preserve; (German): protector, loyal
Wesley: (English & Berman): from the west meadow

Chapter 13. One Syllable Names

When I speak to prospective parents, I tend to hear the same question over and over again: "Why aren't there any great one-syllable names?" This chapter answers that question in a fairly conclusive way: there are dozens of excellent names for boys that are short, sweet, and just one syllable. A better question - how can you choose just one?

Abe: (Jewish): father of nations
Ace: (Latin): unity

Bart: (Hebrew): ploughman; (English): from the barley farm
Beau: (French): handsome, beautiful

Ben: (English): son of my right hand
Black: (English): dark-skinned

Blade: (English): wielding a sword or knife
Blake: (English): pale, fair

Blaze: (Latin): one who stammers; (English): flame
Boone: (French): good

Boyd: (Celtic): blond-haired
Brant: (English): steep, tall

Brent: (English): from the hill
Brett: (French, English & Celtic): a native of Brittany

Brice: (Welsh): alert, ambitious
Brock: (English): badger

Brooks: (English): running water, son of Brooke
Brown: (English): brown color, dark-skinned

Bruce: (French & English): woods, thick brush
Bryce: (Scottish): speckled

Buck: (German & English): male deer
Bud: (English): brotherly

Burke: (German): birch tree
Byrd: (English): bird-like

Cade: (American): pure
Cain: (Israel): craftsman; (Hebrew): spear; (Welsh): clear water; (Irish): archaic

Carl: (English): man; (German): strong one
Cash: (Latin): money

Chad: (English): battle
Chance: (English & French): good luck, keeper of records

Charles: (English): strong, manly
Chase: (English): hunter

Clark: (English): cleric, scholar, clerk
Claude: (English): lame

Claus: (Greek): people's victory
Clay: (English): clay maker, immortal

Cliff: (English): from the ford near the cliff
Clive: (English): one who lives near the cliff

Cole: (Irish): warrior; (English): having dark features
Colt: (American): baby horse; (English): from the dark town

Craig: (Scottish): dwells at the crag; (Welsh): rock
Creed: (English): belief, guiding principle

Dale: (German): valley; (English): lives in the valley
Dane: (Hebrew & Scandinavian): God will judge; (English): brook

Dax: (English & French): water
Dean: (English): head, leader

Dell: (English): from the small valley
Dierks: (Danish): ruler of the people

Dirk: (German): a diminutive form of Derek, which means gifted ruler
Dobbs: (English): fiery

Dolph: (German): diminutive form of Adolph, which means noble wolf
Doyle: (Irish): dark river

Drake: (English): male duck, dragon
Drew/Dru: (English): courageous, valiant

Duane: (Gaelic): a dark and swarthy man
Dwight: (English): a diminutive form of DeWitt, which means blond hair

Earl: (Irish): pledge; (English): nobleman
Fenn: (English): from the marsh

Finn: (English): blond
Fitch: (English): resembling an ermine

Flynn: (Irish): ruddy complexion
Ford: (English): from the river crossing

Fox: (English): fox
Frank: (English): free man

Fred: (German): peaceful ruler
Fynn: (Russian): the Offin River

Gabe: (English): strength of God
Gage/Gaige: (French): a pledge or pawn

Garth: (Scandinavian): keeper of the garden
Gene: (English): a well-born man

George: (English): farmer
Giles: (Greek): resembling a young goat

Gill: (Gaelic): servant
Glenn: (Scottish): glen, valley

Grant: (Latin): great
Gray: (English): gray-haired

Gus: (German): revered
Guy: (French): guide; (Hebrew): valley; (Celtic): sensible; (Latin America): living spirit

Haines: (English): from the vine-covered cottage
Hal: (English): ruler of the army

Hank: (Dutch & German): rules his household
Hans: (German & Hebrew): gift from God; (Scandinavian): God is gracious

Heath: (English): from the heath wasteland
Holt: (English): wood, by the forest

Hoyt: (Irish): mind, spirit
Hugh: (English): intelligent

Hurst: (Irish): dense grove, thicket
Hyde: (English): animal hide

Ike: (Hebrew): full of laughter
Ives: (Scandinavian): the archer's bow

Jack: (English): God is gracious; (Hebrew): supplanter
Jake: (Hebrew): he grasps the heel

James: (English); supplant, replace; (Israel): supplanter
Jan: (Dutch): a form of John, which means God is gracious

Jax: (American): son of Jack
Jay: (German): swift; (French): blue jay; (English): to rejoice; (Latin America): a crow

Jean: (French): a form of John, which means God is gracious
Jess: (Israel): wealthy

Jett: (English): resembling the black gemstone
Jobe: (Hebrew): afflicted

Joel: (Hebrew): Jehovah is God; (Israel): God is willing
John: (Israel): God is gracious; Jehovah has been gracious

Juan: (Hebrew): gift from God; (Spanish): God is gracious
Jules: (French): youthful, downy-haired

Kai: (American): ocean; (Welsh): keeper of the keys; (Scottish): fire
Kale: (English): manly and strong

Kane: (Welsh): beautiful; (Gaelic): little warrior
Karl: (English & Icelandic): man; (French): strong, masculine; (Danish): one who is free

Keefe: (Irish): handsome, loved
Keene: (German): bold, sharp; (English): smart

Keith: (Scottish): wood; (Irish): warrior descending; (Welsh): dwells in the woods
Kent: (English & Welsh): white; (Celtic): chief

King: (English): royal ruler
Kirk: (Norse): a man of the church

Knight: (English): noble soldier
Knox: (English): from the hills

Kris: (Swedish): Christ-bearer
Kurt: (German): brave counselor

Kipp: (English): from the small pointed hill
Kyle: (Gaelic): young; (Irish): young at heart

Lane: (English): narrow road
Laird: (Scottish): lord; (Irish): head of household

Lance: (German): spear; (French): land
Lear: (English): Shakespearean king

Lee/Leigh: (English): meadow
Leif: (Scandinavian): beloved descendent

Lloyd: (Celtic, Welsh & English): gray
Locke: (English): forest

Luke: (Greek & Latin America): light
Lyle: (French & English): from the island

Lynch: (Irish): mariner
Lynn: (English): waterfall

Mark: (Latin): dedicated to Mars, the god of war
Max: (English): greatest

Mead: (English): meadow
Merle: (French): blackbird; (English): falcon

Miles: (German): merciful; (Latin): a soldier
Moore: (French): dark-skinned; (Irish & French): surname

Nash: (American): adventurer
Neal/Neil: (Irish, English & Celtic): a champion

Ned: (English & French): diminutive of Edward, which means wealthy guardian
Niles: (English): champion

Noel: (French): Christmas
North: (English): from the north

Oz: (Hebrew): having great strength
Puck: (English): elf

Pace: (English): a peaceful man
Paine/Payne: (Latin): a peasant

Paul: (English & French): small, apostle in the Bible
Pax: (English): peaceful

Pell: (English): a clerk
Penn: (Latin): pen, quill

Pierce: (English): rock
Platt: (French): flatland

Ponce: (Spanish): fifth
Prince: (Latin): chief, prince

Quinn: (Gaelic): one who provides counsel
Royce: (Irish & French): king, regal; (Scottish, Gaelic & Scottish): red, red-haired

Rafe: (Irish): a tough man
Rain/Raine: (American): blessings from above; (French & Latin): ruler; (English): lord, wise

Ralph: (English): wolf counsel
Rand: (German): the wolf shield

Raul: (French): a form of Ralph, which means wolf counsel
Ray: (French): regal: (Scottish): grace; (English): wise protector

Reed/Reid: (English & French): red-haired
Rex: (Latin): king

Rhett: (English): stream
Rhys/Reese/Reece: (English & Welsh): ardent, fiery, enthusiastic

Rhodes: (Greek): where roses grow
Ridge: (English): from the ridge

Roan: (English): from the Rowan tree
Roark: (Gaelic): champion

Rolf: (German): wolf counsel
Ross: (Scottish): from the peninsula

Saige/Sage: (English & French): wise one; (English): from the spice
Saul: (Israel): borrowed: (Hebrew & Spanish): asked for

Scott: (Scottish): wanderer
Sean/Shawn: (Irish): God is gracious

Seth: (Hebrew): anointed; (Israel): appointed
Shane: (Hebrew): gift from God; (Irish): God is gracious

Shea: (Irish): majestic, fairy place
Slade: (English): child of the valley

Sloan: (English): raid; (Irish, Celtic, Scottish & Gaelic): fighter, warrior
Smith: (English): artisan, tradesman

Stern: (English): austere
Stony: (English): stone

Storm: (English): tempest; (American): impetuous nature
Sven: (Scandinavian): youth

Taft: (French): from the homestead
Thor: (Norse): god of thunder

Thorne: (English): from the thorn bush
Todd: (Scottish): fox

Trent: (Welsh): dwells near the rapid stream
Trey: (English & Latin): third-born child

Trigg: (Norse): truthful
Tripp: (English): traveler

Troy: (French): curly haired; (Irish): foot soldier
True: (English): loyal

Twain: (English): divided in two
Ty: (English): from the fenced-in pasture

Vance: (English): windmill dweller
Vaughn: (Celtic): small

Wade: (English): ford, cross the river
Wayne: (English): craftsman, wagon maker

Webb: (English): weaver
West: (English): from the west

Whit: (English): white-skinned
Wolf: (English): the animal, wolf

Yale: (Welsh): from the fertile upland
Yan/Yann: (Russian): a form of John, which means God is gracious

York: (Celtic, English & Latin America): from the yew tree
Yves: (French): a young archer

Zale: (Greek): having the strength of the sea
Zane: (Hebrew): gift from God; (Arabian): beloved

Zeke: (English): strengthened by God
Zeus: (Greek): powerful one

Chapter 14. Four-Syllable Names

On a practical basis, this chapter is the flip side of Chapter 13, which presents dozens of one syllable names for boys. Here, we will focus on the longest, most elegant and sophisticated names that are at least four syllables. Why, you may ask, would someone choose this type of name for their child, which is hard to pronounce and spell? Many times, a long name is the best fit for a short and simple last name, such as Smith, Tom, Wu, or Lee. Other times, the parents are seeking a formal name that the child can "grow into," such as Alexander. In the meantime, they will call the child one of many possible nicknames, such as Al, Alex, Alec or Zander.

One fascinating aspect about this list: many of these longer names are older, from other cultures, and not particularly common (with a few notable exceptions). Nevertheless, for parents seeking elegant, sophisticated, and mature names that are also somewhat unusual, this chapter has several hidden gems.

Alejandro: (Spanish): defender of mankind
Alexander: (Greek): protector of mankind

Aloysius: (German): famous warrior
Amadeus: (Latin): loves God

Amerigo: (Teutonic): industrious
Arsenio: (Greek): masculine, virile

Archimedes: (Greek): to think about first
Aristotle: (Greek): thinker with a great purpose

Aurelius: (Latin): golden
Azariah: (Hebrew & Israel): God helps

Bartholomew: (English, Hebrew & Biblical): son of a farmer
Bonaventure: (Latin): one who undertakes a blessed venture

Cornelius: (Irish): strong willed, wise; (Latin America): horn-colored
Ezekiel: (Hebrew & Israel): strength of God

Deangelo: (Italian): a combination of De and Angelo; little angel
Demetrius: (Greek): goddess of fertility, one who loves the earth

Ebenezer: (Hebrew & Israel): rock of help
Emmanuel: (Hebrew): God with us

Fabrizio: (Italian): craftsman
Galileo: (Hebrew): one who comes from Galilee

Genovese: (Italian): from Genoa, Italy
Geronimo: (Greek & Italian): a famous chef

Giovanni/Gian: (Italian); God is gracious
Horatio: (French): hour, time

Indiana: (English): from the land of the Indians, the state of Indiana
Macallister: (Gaelic): the son of Alistair

Jedidiah: (Hebrew): one who is loved by God
Jeremiah: (Hebrew): may Jehovah exalt; (Israel): sent by God

Maximilian: (Latin): greatest
Montgomery: (French): rich man's mountain

Napoleon: (French): fierce one
Nehemiah: (Hebrew): compassion of Jehovah

Octavius: (Latin): eighth
Odysseus: (Greek): wrathful

Olivier: (French, English, Danish & Latin America): the olive tree; (German): elf army
Onofrio: (Italian): a defender of peace

Santiago: (Spanish): named for Saint James
Valentino: (Italian): brave or strong; (Latin America): health or love

Zachariah: (Hebrew): Jehovah has remembered; (Israel): remembered by the Lord
Michelangelo*: (Italian): a combination of Michael and Angelo

***Note**: The name Michelangelo is five-syllables, rather than four

Chapter 15. Gender Neutral (Unisex) Names

Throughout this book, you have probably stopped at least once or twice and thought: "Wow, I didn't know *that* was a boy's name." To me, that is the most distinctive trend that is worth noting - the fact that few names are reserved for only one sex.

Fifty years ago, that wasn't the case. If you asked someone to suggest a gender neutral name, they would probably say Pat, Lee, Dale, or Frances - and then draw a blank. Now, there are dozens of popular names that are equally used by both sexes. We've included this chapter for two reasons:

1. to offer suggestions for parents who want a gender neutral name

2. to note the names that truly **are** unisex, for prospective parents who might not be aware of this trend. Sadly, I have met several parents who chose a name on this list, thinking that it was exclusively male. A few years later, they were stunned to learn that there were three little girls in their son's kindergarten class with the same name.

And, that, ultimately, is the only pitfall of unisex names - they don't "announce" your child's gender the way most conventional names do. Nevertheless, these names are definitely hot and trendy - and well worth a second look.

The Top Unisex Names (with gender divisions) from the 2012 Social Security Administration statistics:

1. **Rowan:** (Irish): red-haired; (English & Gaelic): from the rowan tree (37% female)
2. **Quinn:** (Celtic): queenly; (Gaelic): one who provides counsel (68% female)
3. **Kai:** (American): ocean; (Welsh): keeper of the keys; (Scottish): fire (13% female)
4. **Sawyer:** (English): one who works with wood (17% female)
5. **Charlie**: (English) a diminutive form of Charles, which means strong (41% female)
6. **Avery**: (English): wise ruler (81% female)
7. **Finley:** (Irish): blond-haired soldier (66% female)
8. **Elliott:** (Israel): close to God; (English): the Lord is my God (17% female)
9. **Emery:** (German): industrious (80% female)
10. **Emerson:** (English): brave, powerful (61% female)
11. **Rory:** (Irish): famous brilliance, famous ruler; (Gaelic): red-haired (31% female)
12. **Riley:** (English): from the rye clearing; (Irish): a small stream (59% female)
13. **Marlowe:** (English): from the hill by the lake (88% female)
14. **River**: (Latin & French): stream, water (36% female)
15. **Arden:** (English): passionate, enthusiastic, valley of the eagle (74% female)
16. **Peyton:** (English): from the village of warriors (68% female)
17. **Remy:** (French): oarsman or rower, from Rheims (46% female)
18. **Sage:** (English & French): wise one; (English): from the spice (66% female)
19. **Ellis:** (English & Hebrew): my God is Jehovah (35% female)
20. **Addison**: (English): son of Adam (70% female)

A Comprehensive List of Gender Neutral Names (in alphabetical order)

Addison: (English): son of Adam
Alpha: (Greek): first-born child

Aspen: (English): from the aspen tree
Bailey: (English): bailiff, steward, public official

Blair: (Irish & Celtic): from the plain, (Gaelic): child of the fields; (Scottish): peat moss
Blaine: (Gaelic, Irish & Celtic): thin

Blake: (English): pale blond or dark; (Scottish): dark-haired
Blue: (English): the color blue

Brady: (Irish): a large-breasted woman
Brett: (French, English & Celtic): a native of Brittany

Brice/Bryce: (Welsh): alert, ambitious
Camden/Camdyn: (Irish, Scottish, English & Gaelic): from the winding valley

Cameron: (Irish & Gaelic): crooked nose
Campbell: (Gaelic): crooked mouth; (French): from the beautiful field

Cary/Carey: (Greek): pure
Chris: (English & Irish): follower of Christ

Clancy/Clancey: (Celtic): son of the red-haired warrior
Cleo/Clio: (Greek): to praise, acclaim

Coby/Koby/Kobe: (Hebrew): supplanter
Cody: (English): cushion

Corey/Cory: (Irish): from the hollow, of the churning waters
Dale: (German): valley; (English): lives in the valley

Drew: (Greek): courageous, valiant
Derry: (English, Irish, German & Gaelic): red-haired, from the oak grove

Dakota: (Native American): friend to all
Easton: (English): from east town

Ellison: (English): son of Elias
Ellory/Ellery: (Cornish): resembling a swan

Gale/Gail/Gayle: (English): merry, lively
Flynn: (Irish): heir to the red-head; ruddy complexion

Garnet: (English): gem, armed with a spear; (French): keeper of grain
Gentry: (English): gentleman

Hadley: (English & Irish): from the heath covered meadow
Hagen: (Gaelic): youthful

Halsey: (English): Hal's island
Harlow: (English): from the army on the hill

Harper: (English): one who plays or makes harps
Haven: (English): safe place

Hayden: (English): from the hedged valley
Hunter: (English): hunter

Jai: (Tai): heart
Jamie: (Spanish): supplanter

Jensen: (Scandinavian): God is gracious
Jordan: (Hebrew): to flow down; (Israel): descendant

Kacey/Casey: (Irish): brave
Keaton: (English): from the town of hawks

Kelsey: (English): from the island of ships
Kendall: (English & Celtic): from the bright valley

Kent: (English & Welsh): white; (Celtic): chief
Kennedy: (Gaelic): a helmeted chief

Kerry: (Irish): dark-haired
Kim: (Vietnamese): as precious as gold; (Welsh): leader

Kimball: (Greek): hollow vessel
Kinsey: (English): victorious prince

Kirby: (Scandinavian): church village
Kyle: (Irish): attractive

Laine/Lane: (English): narrow road
Lee/Leigh: (English): meadow

Landon: (English): from the long hill
Linden: (English): from linden hill

London/Londyn: (English): capital of England; fortress of the moon
Lynn(e): (English): waterfall

McKenzie: (Irish): fair, favored one
McKinley: (English): offspring of the fair hero

Mika/Micah: (Finnish): like God; (Japanese): new moon
Monroe: (Gaelic): from the red swamp; (Scottish): from the river; (Irish): near the river roe

Morgan: (Celtic): lives by the sea; (Welsh): bright sea
Murphy: (Irish): sea warrior

O'Shea: (Irish): child of Shea
Orion: (Greek): a hunter in Greek mythology

Page/Paige: (French): youthful assistant
Parker: (English): keeper of the park

Paris: (Persian): angelic face; (Greek): downfall; (French): the capital city of France
Pembroke: (Welsh): headland

Presley: (English): priest's land
Quincy: (English): fifth-born child; (French): estate belonging to Quintus

Rain: (American): blessings from above; (Latin): ruler; (English): lord, wise
Reese/Reece: (English & Welsh): ardent, fiery, enthusiastic

Randy: (German): the wolf shield
Rene/Renee: (French): reborn

Rio: (Spanish & Portuguese): river
Rylan/Ryland: (English): the place where rye is grown

Sailor: (American): sailor
Santana: (Spanish): saintly

Shane: (Hebrew): gift from God; (Irish): God is gracious
Shawn: (Irish): a form of Sean, which means God is gracious

Sheridan: (Irish, English & Celtic): untamed; (Gaelic): bright, a seeker
Shiloh: (Hebrew): he who was sent, God's gift, the one to whom it belongs; (Israel): peaceful

Silver: (English): precious metal, the color silver
Sloan: (English): raid; (Irish, Celtic, Scottish & Gaelic): fighter, warrior

Spencer/Spenser: (English): dispenser of provisions
Storm/Stormy: (English): tempest; (American): impetuous nature

Sydney: (English): wide island
Tai: (Chinese): large; (Vietnamese): prosperous

Teagan: (Gaelic): handsome, attractive
Toby: (Hebrew): God is good

Unique: (Latin): only one; (American): unlike others
Whitley: (English): from the white meadow

Chapter 16. Cultural Preferences: Popular Names for African-American Boys

In a country as large and diverse as the United States, parents often choose baby names that honor their cultural heritage and unique family traditions. By doing so, they bring a depth and richness to our society that is fresh and exciting. Other times, parents choose mainstream names that are equally popular among other racial and ethnic groups. We will explore these trends in this chapter by presenting the most popular names for boys in African-American households.

In reading this chapter, please note the source of the data, which prevents us from projecting it to a national level. By design, the Social Security Administration does not break down this information by race; they simply publish the number of times that a name is used across all racial and ethnic groups. Only five states report the information by race: Virginia, Colorado, Arkansas, Texas, and New York. For that reason, we are presenting the top names strictly from those states, in alphabetical order (rather than by popularity). Depending upon where you live - and the level of diversity in your community, these names may (or may not) be particularly common. They do, however, show the amazing range of names that are popular in African-American families in five distinctly different parts of the country.

Aaron: (Jewish): enlightened; (Hebrew): lofty, exalted
Adrian: (German, Spanish & Italian): dark; (Greek): rich

Akil: (Arabian): intelligent
Alonzo: (Spanish & American): ready for battle

Andre: (French): manly, brave
Anel: (Greek): messenger of God, angel

Anthony: (English & Biblical): worthy of praise
Antoine: (French): a flourishing man

Armstrong: (English): strong arm
Barrington: (English): fenced town

Benjamin: (English, Hebrew & Biblical): son of my right hand
Booker: (English): bible, book maker

Caleb: (Israel): faithful; (Hebrew): dog or bold
Calvin: (English & Latin America): bald

Cameron: (Irish & Gaelic): crooked nose
Cassius: (Latin): empty, hollow, vain

Chikae: (African American): God's power
Christian: (English & Irish): follower of Christ

Christopher: (Biblical): Christ-bearer; (English): he who holds Christ in his heart
Cleavon: (English): cliff

Clinton: (English): town on a hill
Cody: (Irish): helpful; (English): a cushion, helpful

Cornelius: (Irish): strong willed, wise; (Latin America): horn-colored
Cory/Corey: (English & Irish): hill, hollow

D'angelo/Deangelo: (Italian): a combination of De and Angelo, which means little angel
D'shawn/Dashawn: (English): God is willing

D'wayne/Dawayne: (Irish): dark, small
Damon: (English): calm, tame

Daniel: (Hebrew & Biblical): God is my judge; (Irish & Welsh): attractive
Darius: (Greek): kingly, wealthy; (American): pharaoh

Darvell: (French): from the eagle town
David: (Hebrew, Scottish & Welsh): beloved

Delroy: (French): belonging to the king
Demarco: (African American): of Mark: (South African): warlike

Demond: (African American): of man
Devin/Devaughn/Devon: (Irish): poet

Dewayne: (American): a combination of De and Wayne, which means wagon maker
Dion: (Greek & French): mountain of Zeus; (African American): God

Dixon: (English): power, brave ruler
Dre: (American): a diminutive form of Andre, which means manly, brave

Edward: (English): wealthy guardian; (German): strong as a boar
Elijah: (Biblical): the Lord is my God; (Hebrew): Jehovah is God

Elon: (Biblical & African American): spirit, God loves me
Emmett/Emmitt: (English): whole, universal

Ennis: (Irish): island; (Gaelic): the only choice; (Greek): mine
Ethan: (Hebrew & Biblical): firm, strong

Gabriel: (Israel): hero of God; (Hebrew): man of God; (Spanish): God is my strength
Garfield: (English): battlefield

Glover: (English): one who makes gloves
Harim/Hareem: (Arabic): superior

Isaiah: (Hebrew): the Lord is generous; (Israel): salvation by God
James: (English): supplant, replace; (Israel): supplanter

Jamal/Jamaal/Jamall/Jamaul: (Arabic): handsome
Jamar: (American): handsome

Jayden: (American): God has heard
Jaylen: (English); to rejoice

Jefferson: (English): son of Jeffrey, which means divine peace
Jeremiah: (Hebrew): may Jehovah exalt; (Israel): sent by God

Jermaine: (French): a man from Germany; (Latin): brotherly
Jordan: (Hebrew): to flow down; (Israel): descendant

Joseph: (Biblical): God will increase; (Hebrew): may Jehovah add/give
Joshua: (Hebrew & Biblical): Jehovah saves

Josiah: (Hebrew): Jehovah has healed; (Israel): God has healed
Justin: (English & French): just, true; (Irish): judicious

Kadeem: (Arabic): servant
Kendrick: (English): royal ruler; (Gaelic): champion

Kenton: (English): from the king's town
Kevin: (Irish & Gaelic): handsome, beautiful; (Celtic): gentle

Kwame: (Akan): born on a Saturday
Lamar: (German): famous land; (French): of the sea

Lamont: (Scandinavian): lawyer
Lance: (German): spear; (French): land

Lashaun: (American): enthusiastic
Levon: (Armenian): lion

Lincoln: (English): Roman colony at the pool; (Latin America): village
Lovell: (French & English): young wolf

Luther: (German): soldier of the people
Malik: (African & Arabic): king, master

Marquis: (French): nobleman
Marvin: (Welsh): friend of the sea

Matthew: (Hebrew & Biblical): gift of the Lord
Michael: (Biblical & Hebrew): like God

Montel: (Italian): mountain
Moses: (Hebrew & Biblical): saved from the water

Nathan: (Hebrew & Israel): gift of God
Nelson: (English, Celtic, Irish & Gaelic): son of Neil

Nero: (Latin & Spanish): stern
Noah: (Biblical): rest, peace; (Hebrew): comfort, long-lived

Omarr: (Arabian): ultimate devotee; (Hebrew): eloquent speaker
Orlando: (Spanish): land of gold: (German): famous throughout the land

Orpheus: (Greek): an excellent musician
Otis: (German & Greek): wealthy

Quashawn: (American): tenacious
Quentin: (Latin): fifth

Quincy: (English): fifth-born child; (French): estate belonging to Quintus
Quinton/Quinten/Quintin: (Latin): from the queen's town

Pearson: (English): son of Peter
Perry: (English): a familiar form of Peter, which means a small stone or rock

Raymone: (Spanish): a wise or mighty protector
Rocket/Rockett/Rockitt: (English): fast

Romeo: (Italian, Spanish, Latin America & African American): from Rome
Roscoe: (Norwegian): deer forest

Rufus: (Latin America): redhead
Samuel: (Israel): God hears; (Hebrew): name of God

Santana: (Spanish): saintly
Sebastian: (Greek): the revered one

Shawn/Shaun: (Irish): a form of Sean, which means God is gracious
Steadman: (English): one who lives at the farm

Stephen/Steven/Stevie: (English & Greek): crowned one
Sylvester/Sly: (Latin): man from the forest

Taye: *(*Ethiopian): one who has been seen
Terrell: (German): thunder ruler

Trenton: (English): town of Trent
Treyvon: (American): a form of Trevon, which is a combination of Trey and Von

Tye/Ty: (English): from the fenced-in pasture
Tyler: (English): maker of tiles

Tyrell: (American & English): thunder ruler
Tyrone/Tyronne: (French): from Owen's land

Tyson: (French): explosive; (English): son of Tye
Vance: (English): windmill dweller

Wardell: (English): from the guardian's hill
Waverly: (English): quaking aspen

Wayan: (Indonesian): first son
Wendall/Wendell: (German): a wanderer

Wesley: (English & German): from the west meadow
Winton: (English): from the enclosed pastureland

William: (English, German & French): protector
Xavier: (Basque): owner of a new house; (Arabic): one who is bright

Zachariah/Zacarias/Zachary: (Hebrew): Jehovah has remembered; (Israel): remembered by the Lord

Chapter 17. Cultural Preferences: Popular Names for Hispanic Boys in the U.S.

On a practical basis, this chapter continues the theme that we started in Chapter 16 - it presents the most popular names for baby boys in Hispanic households in the U.S. (in states that break down this information by race). The selections include a fascinating mix of old and new favorites that blend the richness of the Spanish culture with a decidedly American flair.

In reading this chapter, please note the source of the data, which prevents us from projecting it to a national level. By design, the Social Security Administration does not break down this information by race; they simply publish the number of times that a name is used across all racial and ethnic groups. Only five states report the information by race: Virginia, Colorado, Arkansas, Texas, and New York. For that reason, we are presenting the top names strictly from those states, in alphabetical order (rather than by popularity). Depending upon where you live - and the level of diversity in your community, these names may (or may not) be particularly common. They do, however, show the amazing range of names that are popular in Hispanic families in five distinctly different parts of the country.

Aaron: (Jewish & Hebrew): enlightened
Adrian: (German, Spanish & Italian): dark

Agustin: (Spanish): majestic dignity
Alan: (English & Irish): handsome; (Celtic): harmony, stone or noble

Alejandro: (Spanish): defender of mankind
Alex: (Greek): protector of mankind

Alexander: (Greek): protector of mankind
Alonzo: (Spanish & American): ready for battle

Andres: (Spanish): manly, courageous
Angel: (Spanish & Greek): angelic

Antonio: (Italian & Spanish): a flourishing man, worthy of praise
Axel: (German & Hebrew): father of peace; (German): source of all life

Bautista: (Italian): John the Baptist
Benjamin: (English, Hebrew & Biblical): son of my right hand

Bruno: (German): brown-haired
Caleb: (Israel): faithful; (Hebrew): dog or bold

Carlos: (Spanish): a free man
Che: (Spanish): a derivative of Jose, which means God will add

Christopher: (Biblical): Christ-bearer; (English): he who holds Christ in his heart
Cordero: (Spanish): little lamb

Cristobal: (Spanish): bearer
Cruz: (Spanish): of the cross

Damian: (Greek): one who tames others
Daniel: (Hebrew & Biblical): God is my judge; (Irish & Welsh): attractive

Dante: (Latin): enduring, everlasting
Dario: (Spanish): affluent

David: (Hebrew, Scottish & Welsh): beloved
Diego: (Spanish): Saint James

Dylan: (English & Welsh): born from the ocean, son of the wave; (Gaelic): faithful
Eduardo: (Spanish): wealthy protector or guardian

Elias: (Latin & Hebrew): the Lord is my God
Emiliano: (Italian & Latin): rival, industrious

Emilio: (Spanish): flattering
Emmanuel: (Hebrew): God with us

Enrique: (Spanish): ruler of the estate
Esteban: (Spanish): crowned in victory

Facundo: (Spanish): significant, eloquent
Felipe: (Spanish): one who loves horses

Fernando: (Spanish): daring, adventurous
Francisco: (Spanish): a man from France, free

Franco: (Spanish): frank, free
Gabriel: (Israel): hero of God; (Hebrew): man of God; (Spanish): God is my strength

Gael: (English): merry, lively
Geronimo: (Greek & Italian): a famous chef

Gonzalo:(Spanish): wolf
Hugo: (English): intelligent

Ian: (Scottish): gift from God
Ignacio: (Italian): fiery

Iker: (Spanish): visitation
Isaac: (Biblical): he will laugh

Ivan: (Slavic): God is gracious
Jacobo: (Spanish): supplanter

Javier/Xavier: (Spanish): owner of a new house
Jesus: (Hebrew): God is my salvation

Joaquin: (Hebrew): God will establish
Jorge: (Spanish): farmer

Josue: (Spanish & Hebrew): God is salvation
Juan: (Hebrew): gift from God; (Spanish): God is gracious

Juan David: (Spanish): God is gracious/beloved
Juan Diego: (Spanish): God is gracious/Saint James

Juan Esteban: (Spanish): God is gracious/crowned in victory
Juan Jose: (Spanish): God is gracious/God shall add

Juan Ignacio: (Spanish): God is gracious/fiery
Juan Manuel: (Spanish): God is gracious/like God

Juan Pablo: (Spanish): God is gracious/borrowed
Julian: (Spanish, French & Greek): youthful

Kevin: (Irish & Gaelic): handsome, beautiful; (Celtic): gentle
Lautaro: (Spanish): crowned with laurel

Leonardo: (German): brave as a lion
Lorenzo: (Italian & Spanish): crowned with laurel

Lucas: (Gaelic, English & Latin America): light
Luciano: (Spanish): light

Luis: (Spanish): famous warrior
Manuel: (Spanish): God is with us

Marcos: (Spanish): of mars; (Portuguese): the god of war
Martin: (Latin): dedicated to Mars, the god of war

Mateo: (Italian): gift of God Nicolas:
Matias: (Spanish & Hebrew): gift of God

Matthew: (Hebrew & Biblical): gift of the Lord
Mauricio: (Spanish): moorish; (Portuguese): dark-skinned

Maximiliano: (Italian): greatest
Maximo (Italian): greatest

Miguel: (Spanish): like God
Miguel Angel: (Spanish): like God/angelic

Nicolas: (Greek): victorious people
Pablo: (Spanish): borrowed

Patricio: (Spanish): patrician, noble
Pedro: (Spanish): solid and strong as a rock

Rafael/Raphael: (Spanish): one who is healed by God
Ricardo: (Spanish): strong and powerful ruler

Rodrigo: (Spanish): famous ruler
Sebastian: (Greek): the revered one

Samuel: (Israel): God hears; (Hebrew): name of God
Santiago: (Spanish): named for Saint James

Santino: (Italian): little angel
Salvador: (Spanish & Italian): savior

Simon: (Israel): it is heard
Thiago: (Spanish, Portuguese & Brazilian): Saint James

Tomas: (German): a form of Thomas, which means twin
Vicente: (Spanish): conquering, victorious

Valentino: (Italian): brave or strong; (Latin America): health or love

Chapter 18. Popular Names for Asian Babies

In this chapter, we present the most popular names for Asian-American boys in the last five years (in states that break down this information by race). These eclectic choices, which reflect the amazing history and culture of China, Japan, and Korea, are intriguing options for parents who seek distinctive first and middle names from a traditional part of the world.

In reading this chapter, please note the source of the data, which prevents us from projecting it to a national level. By design, the Social Security Administration does not break down this information by race; they simply publish the number of times that a name is used across all racial and ethnic groups. Only five states report the information by race: Virginia, Colorado, Arkansas, Texas, and New York. For that reason, we are presenting the top names strictly from those states, in alphabetical order (rather than by popularity). Depending upon where you live - and the level of diversity in your community, these names may (or may not) be particularly common. They do, however, show the amazing range of names that are popular in Asian-American families in five distinctly different parts of the country.

Popular Chinese Names for Boys

An: (Chinese): peaceful
Chung: (Chinese): intelligent

Dai: (Chinese): sword technique
Fa: (Chinese): setting off

Fai: (Chinese): beginning to fly
Feng: (Chinese): sharp blade

Gan: (Chinese): dare, adventure
Geming: (Chinese): revolution

Gen: (Chinese): root
Guang: (Chinese): light

He: (Chinese): yellow river
Heng: (Chinese): eternal

Hong: (Chinese): wild swan
Hop: (Chinese): agreeable

Huan: (Chinese): happiness
Hung: (Chinese): brave

Jiang: (Chinese): fire
Jin: (Chinese): gold

Lei: (Chinese): thunder
Li: (Chinese): having great strength

Liang: (Chinese): good man
Liu: (Chinese): one who is quiet and peaceful

Park: (Chinese): the cypress tree
Ping: (Chinese): stable

Qiang: (Chinese): strong
Qiu: (Chinese): autumn

Shan: (Chinese): mountain
Shen: (Chinese): deep spiritual thought

Xiu: (Chinese): cultivated
You: (Chinese): friend

Zhen: (Chinese): astonished
Zian: (Chinese): peace

Popular Japanese Names for Boys

Aki: (Japanese): autumn, bright
Amida: (Japanese): Buddha

Dai: (Japanese): sword technique
Daiki: (Japanese): of great value

Hiro: (Japanese): widespread
Hiromi: (Japanese): widespread beauty; wide-seeing

Isamu: (Japanese): courageous
Isas: (Japanese): meritorious

Jiro: (Japanese): second son
Jo: (Japanese): God will increase

Jun: (Japanese): truthful
Kiyoshi: (Japanese): quiet one

Kuo: (Japanese): approval
Kuro: (Japanese): ninth son

Naoki: (Japanese): honest tree
Naoko: (Japanese): honest

Nobu: (Japanese): faith
Norio: (Japanese): man of principles

Raiden: (Japanese): god of thunder and lightning
Ringo: (Japanese): peace be with you

Ronin: (Japanese): samurai without a master
Shin: (Japanese): truth

Shiro: (Japanese): fourth-born son
Tama: (Japanese): jewel

Popular Korean Names for Boys

Bae: (Korean): inspiration
Chin: (Korean): precious

Cho: (Korean): beautiful
Dae: (Korean): great

Dong: (Korean): the east
Eui: (Korean): righteousness

Eun: (Korean): silver
Hea: (Korean): grace

Hee: (Korean): brightness
Hyo: (Korean): filial duty

Hyun: (Korean): wisdom
Joo: (Korean): jewel

Ki: (Korean): arise
Kwan: (Korean): bold character

Kyong: (Korean): brightness
Kyu: (Korean): standard

Mee: (Korean): beauty
Min: (Korean): cleverness

Nam: (Korean): south
Soo: (Korean): excellent, long life

Yeo: (Korean): mildness
Young: (Korean): forever, unchanging

Chapter 19. Top 10 Names for Boys in Other Countries

Throughout this book, we have focused exclusively on baby names in the United States. For readers with a global perspective, this chapter presents the most popular names for boys in *other* countries. In all cases, the data are taken directly from government statistics for that nation (in the last year that data were available). All names are presented in the order of popularity.

Canada (2011)

1. **Ethan:** (Hebrew & Biblical): firm, strong
2. **Liam**: (Irish & Gaelic): determined protector
3. **Lucas**: (Gaelic, English & Latin America): light
4. **Mason:** (French & English): stone worker
5. **Logan**: (Irish): small cove; (Scottish): Finnian's servant; (Gaelic): from the hollow
6. **Noah:** (Biblical): rest, peace; (Hebrew): comfort, long-lived
7. **Alexander:** (Greek): protector of mankind
8. **Benjamin:** (English, Hebrew & Biblical): son of my right hand
9. **Jacob**: (Biblical): supplanter; (Hebrew): he grasps the heel
10. **Jack:** (English): God is gracious; (Hebrew): supplanter

Australia (2012)

1. **William:** (English, German & French): protector
2. **Lucas**: (Gaelic, English & Latin America): light
3. **Oliver:** (French, English, Danish & Latin America): the olive tree; (German): elf army
4. **Noah:** (Biblical): rest, peace; (Hebrew): comfort, long-lived
5. **Jack:** (English): God is gracious; (Hebrew): supplanter
6. **Ethan:** (Hebrew & Biblical): firm, strong
7. **Lachian**: (Gaelic): war-like
8. **Thomas:** (Hebrew, Greek & Dutch): twin
9. **Joshua:** (Hebrew & Biblical): Jehovah saves
10. **James:** (English): supplant, replace; (Israel): supplanter

Italy (2011)

1. **Francesco**: (Italian): a man from France
2. **Alessandro**: (Greek): defender of man
3. **Andrea**: (Italian): brave
4. **Lorenzo**: (Italian & Spanish): crowned with laurel
5. **Matteo**: (Italian): gift of God
6. **Gabriele:** (Israel): hero of God; (Hebrew): man of God; (Spanish): God is my strength
7. **Mattia**: (Italian): gift of God
8. **Leonardo:** (German): brave as a lion
9. **Davide:** (Hebrew, Scottish & Welsh): beloved
10. **Ricardo**: (Spanish & Italian): strong and powerful ruler

England & Wales (2011)

1. **Harry:** (German): home or house ruler
2. **Oliver:** (French, English, Danish & Latin America): the olive tree; (German): elf army
3. **Jack:** (English): God is gracious; (Hebrew): supplanter
4. **Alfie:** (English): a diminutive form of Alfred, which means elf counselor
5. **Charlie:** (English): a diminutive form of Charles, which means strong, manly
6. **Thomas:** (Hebrew, Greek & Dutch): twin
7. **Jacob:** (Biblical): supplanter; (Hebrew): he grasps the heel
8. **James:** (English): supplant, replace; (Israel): supplanter

9. **Joshua:** (Hebrew & Biblical): Jehovah saves
10. **William:** (English, German & French): protector

France (2010)

1. **Lucas**: (Gaelic, English & Latin America): light
2. **Enzo**: (Italian): ruler of the estate
3. **Leo:** (Italian & English): a lion
4. **Louis:** (French): famous warrior
5. **Hugo:** (English): intelligent
6. **Gabriel:** (Israel): hero of God; (Hebrew): man of God; (Spanish): God is my strength
7. **Ethan:** (Hebrew & Biblical): firm, strong
8. **Mathis:** (English & Greek): a diminutive form of Matthias, which means gift of God
9. **Jules:** (French): youthful, downy-haired
10. **Raphael**: (Spanish): one who is healed by God

Spain (2010)

1. **Alejandro**: (Spanish): defender of mankind
2. **Daniel: (**Hebrew & Biblical): God is my judge; (Irish & Welsh): attractive
3. **Pablo**: (Spanish): a form of Paul, which means small
4. **Hugo:** (English): intelligent
5. **Alvaro**: (Spanish & German): truth-speaker or guardian
6. **Adrian:** (German, Spanish & Italian): dark; (Greek): rich
7. **David:** (Hebrew, Scottish & Welsh): beloved
8. **Diego:** (Spanish): Saint James
9. **Javier**: (Spanish): owner of a new house
10. **Mario:** (Hebrew): bitter, king-ruler

Ireland (2011)

1. **Jack:** (English): God is gracious; (Hebrew): supplanter
2. **James:** (English): supplant, replace; (Israel): supplanter
3. **Sean:** (Irish): God is gracious
4. **Daniel: (**Hebrew & Biblical): God is my judge; (Irish & Welsh): attractive
5. **Conor:** (Irish): strong willed, much wanted
6. **Ryan:** (Gaelic): little king; (Irish): kindly, young royalty
7. **Adam:** (Hebrew): red; (Israel): man of the earth; (English): of the red earth
8. **Harry:** (German): home or house ruler
9. **Michael:** (Biblical & Hebrew): like God
10. **Alex:** (Greek): protector of mankind

Norway (2012)

1. **Emil**: (Latin): eager, industrious
2. **Jonas:** (Hebrew): gift from God; (Spanish): dove; (Israel): accomplishing
3. **William:** (English, German & French): protector
4. **Mathias:** (Spanish & Hebrew): gift of God
5. **Magnus:** (Latin): great
6. **Oliver:** (French, English, Danish & Latin America): the olive tree; (German): elf army
7. **Henrik:** (German): ruler of the home
8. **Elias:** (Latin & Hebrew): the Lord is my God
9. **Liam:** (Irish & Gaelic): determined protector
10. **Adrian:** (German, Spanish & Italian): dark; (Greek): rich

Chapter 20: Names with Similar Meanings

Throughout this book, we have listed the meaning of every name we have presented; we have also presented the same information for each of the 3,000 names in the appendix.

In this chapter, we have summarized a portion of that information for readers who are trying to select a name with a specific meaning. Bear in mind, translations vary widely among languages, which is why we encourage readers to further investigate their top choices, if meanings are important to them. With that in mind, these tables are a general guide to groupings of names that have similar - if not identical - meanings.

Names That Mean "Strong"

Amos	Armstrong	Arnold	Barrett	Bernard	Bogart
Bjorn	Bryan	Carl	Charles	Carlo	Connor
Cornelius	Edward	Ethan	Everett	Harvey	Hartman
Kale	Ken	Jarrett	Malin	Pedro	Ricardo
Quinlan	Richard	Rico	Taurean	Valentino	Virgil

Names That Mean "Brave"

Amos	Andre	Andrew	Bryan	Baldwin	Brendan
Conrad	Devlin	Dixon	Dre	Emerson	Everett
Garcia	Harding	Hardwin	Hillard	Hung	Kurt
Polo	Prewitt				

Names That Mean "Warrior"

Aloysius	Boris	Clancy	Cole	Duncan	Dustin
Gideon	Gunther	Hillard	Keelan	Kane	Keith
Kelly	Lewis	Ludwig	Luigi	Luis	Polo
Mackinley	Malin	Marcel	Murphy	Owen	Sloan

Names That Mean "Noble"

Adolph	Albert	Alan	Alvin	Alphonso	Ansel
Brian	Elgin	Dolph	Earl	Ellsworth	Elmer
Kareen	Knight	Grady	Nolan	Hirum	Odwin
Malloy	Patrick				

Names That Mean "Bright"

Akiko	Albert	Bertram	Colbert	Delbert	Elbert
Englebert	Fulbright	Robert	Robin	Samson	Sheridan
Wilbur	Xavier	Zavier	Minh		

Names That Mean "Dark"

Adrian	Blackwell	Black	Brown	Cole	Dwayne
Delaney	Dolan	Delano	Donal	Douglas	Doyal
Duff	Dugan	Finias	Kerry	Kerwin	Kieran
Maurice	Morrell	Morris	Sullivan		

Names That Mean "Fiery"

Aiden	Dobbs	Egan	Reese	Ignacious	Kagen

Names That Mean "Light"

Abner	Akiko	Alvin	Ashton	Barak	Bertram
Finian	Izod	Lambert	Lucian	Luke	Lux
Lucas	Luka	Orly	Uri		

Names That Mean "Enlightened or Wise"

Aaron	Aryn	Aldo	Alvin	Aldrich	Avery
Cato	Cornelius	Dallas	Reynold	Eldridge	Elvis
Hakin	Rashad	Raymond	Thaddeus	Sage	Socrates

Names That Mean "Beautiful or Handsome"

Adonis	Beauregard	Kane	Keefe	Kevin	Kenneth
Naveen	Jamal	Alan	Bellamy	Hasani	Hussein
Jamar	Japheth	Cullem	Kitoko	McKenna	Teagen

Names That Mean "Peace"

Armani	Axel	Geoffrey	Godfrey	Frederick	Humphrey
Ingram	Jefferson	Pax	Pace	Jeffrey	Manfred
Liu	Noah	Paxton	Salem	Shiloh	Siegfried
Solomon	Wilfred	Zigfred	Ziggy		

Names That Mean "Red"

Adam	Clancy	Derry	Flynn	Flann	Redford
Ridley	Reed	Roden	Rooney	Rory	Rowan
Rufus	Russell	Rusty	Monroe		

Names That Mean "Gift from God"

Hans	Ian	Hansel	Jonas	Johann	Jonathan
Juan	Matteo	Lathan	Nathan	Matthew	Mitchell
Nathaniel	Theodore	Shane	Shiloh	Thierry	Zane

Names That Mean "(God is) Gracious"

Chan	Hans	Elian	Giovanni	Hansel	Jenson
Ioan	Ivan	Jackson	Johann	Jan	Jean
Jock	John	Juan	Yan	Nino	Terrance
Sean	Shane				

Names That Mean "Protector"

Alexander	Alistair	Edmund	Elmo	Fremont	Guillermo
Lex	Liam	Odon	Ramon	Raymond	Zander
Sacha	Sigmund	Warren	William		

Names That Mean "Champion or Victorious"

Carlin	Carroll	Kendrick	Neal	Nigel	Roark
Ajay	Vijay	Kinsey	Nicholas	Niles	Nicolai
Seigfried	Sigmund	Victor	Vincent	Zigfred	Ziggy

Names That Mean "Joy or Happy"

| Alaire | Asher | Winston | Denton | Felix | Sayed |

Names That Mean "Sun"

| Apollo | Helio | Ravi | Samson |

Names That Mean "Supplanter"

| Coby | Jack | Iago | Jacques | Jacob | Jamie |
| James | Kobe | Kemo | Seamus | | |

Names That Mean Defender

| Alejandro | Azim | Eli | Hero | Titus | Onofrio |
| Warner | Zander | | | | |

Names That Mean Intelligent

| Akira | Chung | Hakin | Hewitt | Hugh | Keene |
| Hobart | Hubert | Fulbright | Akilah | Tomo | Trang |

Names Relating "To The Sea"

Hurley	Lamar	Marlon	Marvin	Merlin	Merrick
Merrill	Morgan	Mortimer	Murdoch	Murphy	Neptune
Ocean	Seaman	Seaton	Zale		

Chapter 21: Names that Sound Alike

Many times, parents disagree on a potential name for superficial reasons:

- it is too popular
- the initials don't work
- their sister, best friend, or cousin is planning to use the same name
- a bad connotation (i.e., the name elicits memories of a professional rival, childhood bully, or former romantic partner)

Often, the solution to this dilemma is choosing a name that *rhymes* with the original - it has a similar sound and feel, without the negative "baggage." This chapter presents several combinations of boys" names that rhyme. If you like one - but you can't persuade your partner to choose it, see if (s)he likes the other........

Aaron: (Jewish & Hebrew): enlightened
Darren: (English, Irish & Gaelic): great

Alvin: (Germany): light skin, noble friend; (English): wise friend
Calvin: (English & Latin America): bald

Barrett: (English & German): strength of a bear
Garrett: (Irish): to watch

Bryan: (Irish): strong one; (Celtic): brave
Ryan: (Gaelic): little king; (Irish): kindly, young royalty

Chance: (English & French): good luck, keeper of records
Lance: (Germany): spear; (French): land

Cody: (Irish): helpful; (English): a cushion, helpful
Brody: (Irish): brother, from the muddy place; (Scottish): second son

Dustin: (English): fighter, warrior
Justin: (English & French): just, true; (Irish): judicious

Devon: (English & Irish): a poet, a county in England
Kevin: (Irish & Gaelic): handsome, beautiful; (Celtic): gentle
Evan: (English): God is good; (Welsh): young; (Celtic): young fighter

Donald: (Celtic & Gaelic): dark stranger; (Irish, English & Scottish): great leader
Arnold: (German): strong as an eagle
Ronald: (English, Gaelic & Scottish): rules with counsel

Eric: (Scandinavian): honorable ruler
Derek: (German & English): gifted ruler

Frank: (Latin America): free
Hank: (Dutch & German): rules his household

Hogan: (Irish & Gaelic): young, young at heart
Logan: (Irish): small cove; (Scottish): Finnian's servant; (Gaelic): from the hollow

Kyle: (Gaelic): young; (Irish): young at heart
Lyle: (French & English): from the island

Jason: (Greek): to heal
Mason: (French & English): stone worker

Sean/Shawn: (Irish): God is gracious
John: (Israel): God is gracious; Jehovah has been gracious

Taylor: (English & French): a tailor
Tyler: (English): tile maker

Barry: (English & Irish): fair-haired; (Celtic); marksman; (Gaelic): spear
Harry: (German): home or house ruler
Larry: (Dutch & Latin America): laurels

Jordan: (Hebrew): to flow down; (Israel): descendant
Aiden: (Irish, Celtic & Gaelic): fire, fiery
Hayden: (English): the rosy meadow
Cayden: (Scottish): fighter
Jayden: (American): God has heard

Appendix: Alphabetical List of Boys Names

Aaron: (Jewish): enlightened; (Hebrew): lofty, exalted
Abbott: (Hebrew): father
Abdul: (Arabic): servant of God
Abe: (Jewish): father of nations
Abel: (Hebrew & Biblical): breathe, son
Abner: (Israel & Hebrew): father is light, father of light
Abraham: (Hebrew & Biblical): exalted father
Abram: (Hebrew): high father; (Israel): father of nations
Abu: (African): father
Ace: (Latin): unity
Achilles: (Greek): hero of the Trojan War
Ackerly: (English): meadow of oak trees
Adair: (Scottish): oak tree ford
Adalius: (German) : noble
Adam: (Hebrew): red; (Israel): man of the earth; (English): of the red earth
Adamson: (English): the son of Adam
Addison: (English): son of Adam
Adler: (German): eagle
Adolf/Adolph: (German): noble wolf
Adonis: (Greek): beautiful
Adrian: (German, Spanish & Italian): dark; (Greek): rich
Adriel: (Hebrew): from God's flock
Agustin: (Spanish): majestic dignity
Ahmad: (Arabic): one who thanks God
Ahman: (Arabic): a derivative of Ahmad, which means one who thanks God
Ahmet: (Turkish): worthy of praise
Aidan/Aiden/Adan: (Irish, Celtic & Gaelic): fire, fiery
Aiken: (English): sturdy, made of oak
Ainsley: (Scottish): my own meadow
Ainsworth: (English): from Ann's estate
Ajax: (Greek): warrior
Ajay: (Punjabi): victorious, undefeatable
Ajit: (Indian): invincible
Akeem: (Hebrew): a form of Joachim, which means God will establish
Aki: (Japanese): autumn, bright
Akiko: (Japanese): surrounded by bright light
Akil: (Arabian): intelligent
Akira: (Japanese): intelligent
Aladdin: (Arabian): faithful
Alaire: (French): filled with joy
Alan/Allan/Allen: (English & Irish): handsome; (Celtic): harmony, stone or noble
Alastair: (Scottish): a form of Alexander, which means protector of mankind
Albert/Alberto: (English & German): noble, bright
Alden: (English): old, wise protector
Aldo: (German): old and wise
Aldrich: (English): wise counselor
Alejandro: (Spanish): defender of mankind
Alessandro: (Greek): defender of man
Alexander/Alex/Alek/Alexi/Alexis: (Greek): protector of mankind
Alfonso/Alfonzo: (Italian): ready for battle
Alfred: (English): elf counselor
Alfie: (English): a diminutive form of Alfred, which means elf counselor
Alistair/Allister: (English): a form of Alexander, which means protector of mankind
Alon: (Hebrew): of the oak tree

Alonzo: (Spanish & American): ready for battle
Aloysius: (German): famous warrior
Alpha: (Greek): first-born child
Alphonso/Alphonse: (Italian & German): noble and eager
Altair: (Greek): star
Alton: (English): from the old town
Alvaro: (Spanish & German): truth-speaker or guardian
Alvin: (German): light skin, noble friend; (English): wise friend
Amadeus: (Latin): loves God
Amal: (Hebrew): worker; (Arabic): hopeful
Amani: (African): peaceful
Amare: (African): handsome
Amber: (French): amber
Ambrose: (Greek): immortal
Amerigo: (Teutonic): industrious
Ames: (French): friend
Amida: (Japanese): Buddha
Amil: (Hindu): invaluable
Amir: (Arabic): prince
Amit: (Arabic): highly praised
Ammon: (Egyptian): god of a unified Egypt
Amory: (German): ruler
Amos: (Hebrew): strong, carried, brave: (Israel): troubled
An: (Chinese & Vietnamese): peaceful
Anders: (Scandinavian): a courageous, valiant man
Anderson: (Scottish): son of Andrew
Andre: (French): manly, brave
Andrea: (Italian): brave
Andrei: (Italian): manlike
Andres: (Spanish): manly, courageous
Andrew: (English, Scottish & Biblical): manly; brave
Anel: (Greek): messenger of God, angel
Angel: (Spanish & Greek): angelic
Angelo: (Italian): angel
Angus: (Irish): vigorous one
Anil: (Hindu): wind god
Ansel: (French): follower of a nobleman
Anson: (German): divine
AnthonyAntony: (English & Biblical): worthy of praise
Antoine/Anton: (French): a flourishing man
Antonio: (Italian & Spanish): a flourishing man, worthy of praise
Antwan/Antwaun/Antwoine/Antwon/Antwone: (Arabic): worthy of praise
Anwar: (Arabic): luminous
Apollo: (Latin): strength, sun god
Apollos: (Israel): one who destroys
Archer: (Latin): a skilled bowman
Archibald: (German): bold
Archimedes: (Greek): to think about first
Arden: (Latin): passionate
Ares: (Greek): god of war
Aristotle/Ari: (Greek): thinker with a great purpose
Arlen: (Irish): pledge
Arlo: (Spanish): barberry
Armand/Armando: (French): of the army
Armani/Armon: (Hebrew): high fortress
Armstrong: (English): strong arm

Arne/Arnie/Arnold: (German): strong as an eagle
Arroyo: (Spanish): irrigation channel
Arsenio: (Greek): masculine, virile
Arthur/Art/Artur/Arturo: (English): bear, stone
Ary: (Hebrew): lion of God
Aryn: (Hebrew & Arabic): a form of Aaron, which means enlightened
Asa: (Hebrew): physician; Japan: born at dawn
Asante: (African): thank you
Ash/Ashe: (English): tree
Ashby: (Scandinavian): ash tree farm
Asher: (Hebrew & Israel): happy, blessed
Ashley: (English & Biblical): lives in the ash tree
Ashton: (Hebrew): shining light; (English): ash tree settlement
Atlas: (Greek): lifted, carried
Atticus: (Latin): a man from Athens
Attila: (Gothic): little father
Atwell: (English): one who lives at the spring
Aubrey: (English): one who rules with elf-wisdom
Auburn: (Latin): reddish-brown
Augustine/August/Augie/Augustus: (German): revered
Aurelius: (Latin): golden
Austin/Austen: (English): from the name Augustin, which means revered
Avery: (English): wise ruler
Avi: (Hebrew): my God, father; (Latin America): Lord of mine
Axel/Axl: (German & Hebrew): father of peace; (German): source of all life
Azariah: (Hebrew & Israel): God helps
Azim: (Arabic): defender

Baden: (German): bather
Bae: (Korean): inspiration
Bailey: (French): bailiff, steward
Bain: (Irish): fair-haired
Bainbridge: (Irish): fair bridge
Baird: (Irish): traveling minstrel
Baldwin: (German): brave friend
Balthazar: (English): the comedy of errors a merchant
Bancroft: (English): from the bean field
Barak: (Hebrew & Israel): flash of lightening
Barclay: (Scottish & English): birch tree meadow
Barlow: (English): bare hillside
Barnabus: (Hebrew & Israel): comfort
Barnett: (English): of honorable birth
Barney: (English): comfort
Baron: (English): a title of nobility
Barr: (English): a lawyer
Barrett: (German): strong as a bear
Barrington: (English): fenced town
Barry: (English & Irish): fair-haired; (Celtic); marksman; (Gaelic): spear
Bart: (Hebrew): ploughman; (English): from the barley farm
Bartholomew: (English, Hebrew & Biblical): son of a farmer
Bartlett: (French): son of the father
Barton: (English): from the barley town
Basil: (Greek & Latin): royal, kingly
Bautista: (Italian): John the Baptist

Baxter: (English): baker
Bay: (Vietnamese): born on a Saturday; (American): a natural body of water
Beacan: (Irish): small
Beau: (French): handsome, beautiful
Beaufort: (French): beautiful fort
Beaumont: (French): beautiful mountain
Beauregard: (French): handsome, beautiful
Beck: (English): the brook
Becker: (German): baker
Beckett/Beck: (English) : brook
Beckham: (Englidh): from the Beck homestead
Beethoven: (German): music
Bellamy: (French): handsome
Ben: (English): son of my right hand
Benedict: (Latin): Blessed
Benito: (Italian): blessed
Benjamin: (English, Hebrew & Biblical): son of my right hand
Bennett: (English): one who is blessed
Benoit: (French): bland
Benson: (English): son of Benedict
Bentley: (English): from the bent grass meadow
Beowulf: (English): intelligent wolf
Beresford: (English): from the barley ford
Bergen: (German): hill lover
Berkeley: (English & Irish): from the birch meadow
Bernard: (German): strong as a bear
Bertram/Bert: (German & English): bright light
Bevis: (Teutonic): an archer
Bing: (German): kettle-shaped hollow
Birch: (English): white, shining
Birkitt: (English): birch-tree coast
Birney: (English): from the island with the brook
Bjorn: (Scandinavian): a form of Bernard, which means strong as a bear
Black: (English): dark-skinned
Blackwell: (English): from the dark spring
Blade: (English): wielding a sword or knife
Blaine: (Gaelic, Irish & Celtic): thin
Blair: (Irish): plain, field
Blaise: (French & English): stutter, stammer
Blake: (English): pale, fair
Blaze: (Latin): one who stammers; (English): flame
Bodhi: (Indian): awakens
Bogart: (French): strong with a bow
Bonaventure: (Latin): one who undertakes a blessed venture
Booker: (English): bible, book maker
Boone: (French): good
Boris: (Slavic): warrior
Boston: (English): the city Boston
Bowen: (Gaelic): small son; (Irish): archer
Bowie: (Celtic): yellow-haired
Boyd: (Celtic): blond-haired
Bracken: (English): resembling a large fern
Braden/Brayden/Braiden: (Irish & English): broad hillside; (Scottish): salmon
Braddock: (English); from the broadly spread oak
Bradford: (English): from the wide ford

Bradman: (English): the foreman of Brad
Brady: (Gaelic & Irish): spirit; (Irish): broad-shouldered
Brandon: (Irish): little raven
Branson/Bransen: (English): the son of Brandon
Brant/Brantley: (English): steep, tall
Braxton: (English): from Brock's town
Breck: (Irish): freckled
Brendan: (Irish): prince; (Gaelic): brave; (Celtic & Irish): raven; (German): flame
Brennan: (Gaelic): teardrop
Brent: (English): from the hill
Bret/Brett: (French, English & Celtic): a native of Brittany
Brian: (Gaelic): noble birth; (Celtic): great strength
Brice: (Welsh): alert, ambitious
Brigham: (English): covered bridge
Britt/Britton/Brittan: (Scottish): from Britain
Brock: (English): badger
Broderick: (English): from the wide ridge
Brody: (Irish): brother, from the muddy place; (Scottish): second son
Brogan: (Gaelic & Irish): from the ditch
Bronson: (English): son of Brown
Brooks: (English): running water, son of Brooke
Brown: (English): brown color, dark-skinned
Bruce: (French & English): woods, thick brush
Bruno: (German): brown-haired
Brutus: (Latin): course, stupid
Bryan: (Irish): strong one; (Celtic): brave
Bryce: (Scottish): speckled
Bryson: (American): son of a nobleman
Buck: (German & English): male deer
Buckley: (English): deer meadow
Bud: (English): brotherly
Budha: (Hindu): the planet Mercury
Buford: (English): ford near the castle
Burgess: (English): town dweller, shopkeeper
Burke: (German): birch tree
Burton: (English): from the fortified town
Butler: (English): keeper of the bottles
Byrd: (English): bird-like
Byron: (French & English): barn or cottage

Cade: (American): pure
Caden: (Welsh): spirit of battle
Caesar: (Latin): emperor
Caiden/Caden: (American): friend, companion
Cain: (Israel): craftsman; (Hebrew): spear; (Welsh): clear water; (Irish): archaic
Caleb: (Israel): faithful; (Hebrew): dog or bold
Callan/Callen: (Australian): sparrow hawk
Callum: (Gaelic): resembling a dove
Calvin: (English & Latin America): bald
Camden: (Irish, Scottish, English & Gaelic): from the winding valley
Cameron: (Irish & Gaelic): crooked nose
Campbell: (Gaelic): crooked mouth; (French): from the beautiful field
Carey: (Greek): pure
Carl/Carle: (English): man; (German): strong one
Carlin: (Irish, Gaelic & Scottish): little champion
Carlisle: (English): from the walled city

Carlo: (French): strong; (Italian): manly
Carlos: (Spanish): a free man
Carlsen: (Scandinavian): son of Carl
Carlton/Carleton: (English): town of Charles
Carlyle: (English): Carl's island
Carmelo: (Hebrew & Israel): fruit orchard
Carmine: (Latin): beautiful song
Carroll: (Irish): champion
Carson: (English): son who lives in the swamp
Carter: (English): cart driver
Carver: (English): sculptor
Cary: (Celtic): from the river; (Welsh): from the fort on the hill
Cash: (Latin): money
Casper: (Persian): treasurer; (German): imperial
Cassius: (Latin): empty, hollow, vain
Castor: (Greek): bereaved brother of Helen
Cato: (Latin): sagacious, wise one, good judgment
Caton: (Spanish): knowledgeable
Cayden: (Scotland): fighter
Ceasar/Caesar: (Latin): long-haired
Cecil: (Latin): blind
Cedric: (English): battle chieftain
Chad: (English): battle
Chadwick: (English): from Chad's dairy farm
Chai: (Hebrew): giver of life
Chan: (Spanish): God is gracious
Chance: (English & French): good luck, keeper of records
Chancellor/Chancelor/Chancey: (English): record keeper
Chandler: (French): candle maker
Channing: (French): church official; (English): resembling a young wolf
Charles: (English): strong, manly
Chase: (English): hunter
Chauncey: (Latin): chancellor
Chavez: (Spanish): a surname
Che: (Spanish): a derivative of Jose, which means God will add
Chen: (Chinese): great, dawn
Chester: (English): a rock fortress
Chevy: (French): a diminutive form of Chevalier, which means horseman, knight
Chico: (Spanish): boy
Chikae: (African American): God's power
Chin: (Korean): precious
Chip: (English): chipping sparrow
Cho: (Korean): beautiful
Christian: (English & Irish): follower of Christ
Christopher/Christoff: (Biblical): Christ-bearer; (English): he who holds Christ in his heart
Chun: (Chinese): spring
Chung: (Chinese): intelligent
Cicero: (Latin): chickpea
Ciro: (Italian): a diminutive form of Cyril, which means lordly
Cisco: (Spanish): a diminutive form of Francisco, which means free
Clancy/Clancey: (Celtic): son of the red-haired warrior
Clarence: (English & Latin America): clear, luminous
Clark: (English): cleric, scholar, clerk
Claud/Claude: (English): lame
Claudius: (English): lame
Claus: (Greek): people's victory

Clay: (English): clay maker, immortal
Clayborne: (English): brook near the clay pit
Clayton: (English): mortal
Cleavon: (English): cliff
Clement: (French): compassionate
Cleo: (Greek): to praise, acclaim
Cletus: (Greek): illustrious
Cliff/Clifford/Clifton: (English): from the ford near the cliff
Clinton: (English): town on a hill
Clive: (English): one who lives near the cliff
Clyde: (Irish): warm
Coburn: (English): meeting of streams
Coby: (English): supplanter
Cody: (Irish): helpful; (English): a cushion, helpful
Colbert: (French): famous and bright
Cole: (Irish): warrior; (English): having dark features
Colin/Collin: (Irish & Gaelic): young; (Scottish): young dog; (English): of a triumphant people
Colt: (American): baby horse; (English): from the dark town
Colton: (English): coal town, from the dark town
Columbus: (Greek): curious
Conan: (English): resembling a wolf; (Gaelic): high and mighty
Cong: (Chinese): clever
Conlan: (Irish): hero
Connery: (Scottish): daring
Connor/Conner: (Irish): strong willed, much wanted
Conrad: (German): brave counselor
Constantine: (Latin): steadfast, firm
Cooper: (English): barrel maker
Corbett: (French): resembling a young raven
Cordero: (Spanish): little lamb
Cornelius: (Irish): strong willed, wise; (Latin America): horn-colored
Cory/Corey: (English & Irish): hill, hollow
Cosimo: (Italian): the order of the universe
Cosmo: (Greek): the order of the universe
Covington: (English); from the town near the cave
Coy/Coye/Coyt: (English): woods
Craig: (Scottish): dwells at the crag; (Welsh): rock
Cramer: (English): full
Crandall: (English): from the valley of cranes
Crawford: (English): from the crow's ford
Creed: (English): belief, guiding principle
Creighton: (Scottish): from the border town
Crispin: (Latin): curly-haired
Cristobal: (Spanish): bearer
Cromwell: (English): winding spring
Crosby: (English): town crossing
Cruz: (Spanish): of the cross
Cuba: (Spanish): tub
Cullen: (Irish & Gaelic): handsome; (Celtic): cub; (English): city in Germany
Culley: (Irish): woods
Culver: (English): dove
Cunningham: (Gaelic): descendant of the chief
Curran/Curry: (Celtic): hero
Curtis: (Latin): enclosure
Cutter: (English): tailor
Cyrano: (Greek): from Cyrene

Cyril: (English & Greek): master, lord
Cyrus: (English): far-sighted

Dack: (English): from the French town of Dax
Dae: (Korean): great
Daegan: (Irish): black-haired
Dai: (Chinese): sword technique
Daiki: (Japanese): of great value
Dakota: (Native American): friend to all
Dale: (German): valley; (English): lives in the valley
Dallas: (Irish & Gaelic): wise; (Scottish & Celtic): from the waterfall
Dalton: (English): from the town in the valley
Damian: (Greek): one who tames others
Damon: (English): calm, tame
Dane: (Hebrew & Scandinavian): God will judge; (English): brook
Daniel: (Hebrew & Biblical): God is my judge; (Irish & Welsh): attractive
Dante: (Latin): enduring, everlasting
Darian: (Irish): from the name Darren, which means great
Dario: (Spanish): affluent
Darius: (Greek): kingly, wealthy; (American): pharaoh
Darnel/Darnell: (English): hidden
Darren/Darrin/Darin/Darron/Darryn: (English, Irish & Gaelic): great
Darvell: (French): from the eagle town
Darwin/Derwin: (English): dear friend
Daryl/Darrell: (French): darling, beloved
Dashawn: (English): God is willing
Dashiell: (French): page boy
David: (Hebrew, Scottish & Welsh): beloved
Davis: (English & Scottish): David's son
Dawayne/Dwayne: (Irish): dark, small
Dawson: (English): son of David
Dax: (English & French): water
De: (Chinese): virtuous
Deacon: (American): pastor; (English): dusty one, servant
Dean: (English): head, leader
Deangelo: (Italian): a combination of De and Angelo, which means little angel
Decker: (German): one who prays: (Hebrew): piercing
Declan: (Irish): saint
Dedrick: (German): ruler of the people
Deepak: (Hindu): little lamp
Deion/Dion/Deiondre: (Greek & French): mountain of Zeus
Delaney: (Irish): dark challenger
Delano: (English): nut tree; (Irish): dark
Delbert: (English): proud, bright as day
Dell: (English): from the small valley
Delroy: (French): belonging to the king
Demarco: (African American): of Mark: (South African): warlike
Demetrius: (Greek): goddess of fertility, one who loves the earth
Demond: (African American): of man
Dennis: (Greek): wild, frenzied
Dennison: (English): son of Dennis
Denton: (English): happy home
Denzel: (English): fort; (African): wild
Derby: (English): deer park; (Irish): from the village of dames
Derek: (German & English): gifted ruler
Dermot: (Irish): free from envy

Derry: (English, Irish, German & Gaelic): red-haired, from the oak grove
Deshawn/Deshaun: (American): a combination of De and Shawn, which means God is gracious
Desi: (Latin): desiring
Desmond: (Gaelic): a man from South Munster
Destin: (French): fate
Devin/Devaughn/Devon: (Irish): poet
Devlin: (Gaelic): fierce bravery
Dewayne: (American): a combination of De and Wayne, which means wagon maker
Dewey: (Welsh): prized
DeWitt: Flemish: blond hair
Dexter: (Latin): right-handed, skillful; (Latin America): flexible
Diego: (Spanish): Saint James
Diego Alejandro: (Spanish): Saint James/defender of mankind
Dierks: (Danish): ruler of the people
Diesel: (American): having great strength
Dietrich: (German): ruler of the people
Dijon: (French): a city in France
Dimitri/Demetrius: (Russian): lover of the earth
Dino: (Italian): one who wields a great sword
Dirk: (German): a diminutive form of Derek, which means gifted ruler
Dixon: (English): power, brave ruler
Dobbs: (English): fiery
Dolan: (Irish): dark-haired
Dolph: (German): diminutive form of Adolph, which means noble wolf
Domingo: (Spanish): born on a Sunday
Dominic: (Spanish): born on a Sunday
Donal/Donald: (Celtic & Gaelic): dark stranger; (Irish, English & Scottish): great leader
Dong: (Korean): the east
Donovan: (Irish): brown-haired chief
Doug/Dougal/Douglas: (Scottish): dark river
Doyle: (Irish): dark river
Drake: (English): male duck, dragon
Draper: (English): fabric maker
Dre: (American): a diminutive form of Andre, which means manly, brave
Drew/Dru: (English): courageous, valiant
Driscoll: (Celtic): mediator
Drummond: (Scottish): one who lives near the ridge
Drury: (French): loving
Dryden: (English): dry valley
Duane: (Gaelic): a dark and swarthy man
Dudley: (English): common field
Duff: (Scottish): dark
Dugan: (Irish): dark
Duke: (English): leader
Duncan/Dunn: (Scottish): brown warrior
Dustin/Dusty: (English): fighter, warrior
Dwayne: (Irish): dark
Dwight: (English): a diminutive form of DeWitt, which means blond hair
Dylan/Dillon/Dilan: (English & Welsh): born from the ocean, son of the wave; (Gaelic): faithful

Eagle: (Native American): resembling the bird
Eamon: (Irish): blessed guardian
Earl: (Irish): pledge; (English): nobleman
Earnest: (English): industrious

Eastman: (English): a man from the east
Easton: (English): from east town
Eben: (Hebrew): rock
Ebenezer: (Hebrew & Israel): rock of help
Edgar: (English): powerful and wealthy spearman
Edison: (English): son of Edward
Edmund/Edmond: (English): wealthy protector
Eduardo: (Spanish): wealthy protector or guardian
Edward: (English): wealthy guardian; (German): strong as a boar
Edwin: (English): wealthy friend
Efrain/Ephraim: (Hebrew): fruitful
Egan/Egin/Egen/Egyn: (Irish): ardent, fiery
Elan: (Hebrew): tree
Elbert: (English): a well-born man; (German): a bright man
Eldon: (English): from the sacred hill
Eldridge: (German & English): wise ruler
Elgin: (English) & Celtic): noble, white
Eli/Ely: (Hebrew): ascended, uplifted, high; (Greek): defender of man
Elian: (Spanish): consecrated to the gracious God
Elias: (Latin & Hebrew): the Lord is my God
Elijah: (Biblical): the Lord is my God; (Hebrew): Jehovah is God
Elliott: (Israel): close to God; (English): the Lord is my God
Ellis: (English & Hebrew): my God is Jehovah
Ellison: (English): son of Elias
Ellory/Ellery: (Cornish): resembling a swan
Ellsworth: (English): from the nobleman's estate
Elmer: (English): famous, noble
Elmo: (English): protector; (Latin): amiable
Elmore: (English): moor where the elm trees grow
Elon: (Biblical & African American): spirit, God loves me
Elroy: (French, English & African American): king; (Irish): red-haired youth
Elton: (English): old town
Elvin: (Irish): friend of elves
Elvis: (Scandinavian): wise
Elwood: (English): old forest
Emerson: (English): brave, powerful
Emery: (German): industrious leader
Emil/Emile: (Latin): eager, industrious
Emiliano: (Italian & Latin): rival, industrious
Emilio: (Spanish): flattering
Emmanuel: (Hebrew): God with us
Emmett/Emmitt: (English): whole, universal
Engelbert: (German): bright as an angel
Ennis: (Irish): island; (Gaelic): the only choice; (Greek): mine
Enoch: (Hebrew): dedicated, consecrated
Enos: (Hebrew): man
Enrique: (Spanish): ruler of the estate
Enzo: (Italian): ruler of the estate
Ephraim: (Hebrew & Israel): fruitful
Eric/Erik/Erich: (Scandinavian): honorable ruler
Ernest: (German): serious, determined, truth
Errol: (Latin): wanderer
Esau: (Hebrew): hairy, famous bearer; (Israel): he that acts or finishes
Esme: (French): esteemed
Esteban: (Spanish): crowned in victory

Ethan: (Hebrew & Biblical): firm, strong
Eugene: (Greek): well-born man
Eui: (Korean): righteousness
Eun: (Korean): silver
Evan: (English): God is good; (Welsh): young; (Celtic): young fighter
Evander: (Greek): benevolent ruler
Everett: (English): hardy, brave, strong
Ewan: (Celtic, Scotch & Irish): young
Ezekiel: (Hebrew & Israel): strength of God
Ezra: (Hebrew & Israel): helper

Fa: (Chinese): setting off
Fabian/Faber/Fabio: (Latin): bean grower
Fabrizio/Fabrice: (Italian): craftsman
Facundo: (Spanish): significant, eloquent
Fagan/Fagin: (Gaelic): ardent; (Irish): eager
Fai: (Chinese): beginning to fly
Fairbanks: (English): from the bank along the path
Faisal: (Arabic): decisive
Falkner: (English): trainer of falcons
Fargo: (American): jaunty
Farley: (English): bull meadow
Farnell: (English): fern-covered hill
Farrell/Ferrell: (Irish): heroic, courageous
Farrow: (English): piglet
Faust: (Latin): fortunate
Felipe: (Spanish): one who loves horses
Felix: (Latin): happy and prosperous
Felton: (English): from the town near the field
Feng: (Chinese): sharp blade
Fenn: (English): from the marsh
Fenton: (English): from the farm on the fens
Ferdinand: (German): courageous voyager
Fergus: (Gaelic): first and supreme choice
Fernando: (Spanish): daring, adventurous
Ferris: (Irish): small rock
Fidel: (Latin) faithful
Fielding: (Irish): from the field
Filbert: (English): brilliant
Finch: (Irish): resembling the small bird
Fineas/Phineas: (Egyptian): dark-skinned
Finian/Phinian: (Irish): light-skinned, white
Finlay/Findlay/Finian/Finley: (Irish): blond-haired soldier
Finn: (English): blond
Finnegan: (Irish): fair-haired
Fisher: (English): fisherman
Fitch: (English): resembling an ermine
Fitzgerald: (English) the son of Gerald
Fitzpatrick: (English): son of Patrick
Flann: (Irish): redhead
Fleming: (English): from Denmark
Fletcher: (English): one who makes arrows
Flint: (English): stream, hard quartz rock
Flynn: (Irish): ruddy complexion; heir to the red-head
Fogarty: (Irish): exiled
Foley: (English): creative

Fontaine: (French): from the water source
Ford: (English): from the river crossing
Forrest: (English & French): from the woods
Forster: (American & French): from the woods
Foster: (English & French): one who keeps the forest
Fox: (English): fox
Francesco: (Italian): a man from France
Francis/Franco: (Latin): a man from France
Francisco: (Spanish): a man from France, free
Franco: (Spanish): frank, free
Frank/ Frankie/Franklin: (English): free man
Franz/Frantz: (German): a man from France
Fraser: (Scottish): strawberry flowers
Frasier: (French): strawberry, curly-haired
Fred: (German): peaceful ruler
Frederick/Frederique/Frederico/Freidrich: (German): peaceful ruler
Freeborn: (English): child of freedom
Freeman: (English): free
Fremont: (French): protector of freedom
Frey: (English): lord
Frick: (English): bold
Fulbright: (English): brilliant
Fuller/Fullerton: (English): from Fuller's town
Fyfe: (Scottish): a man from Fifeshire
Fynn: (Russian): the Offin River

Gabe: (English): strength of God
Gabriel: (Israel): hero of God; (Hebrew): man of God; (Spanish): God is my strength
Gaetan: (French & Italian): from Italy
Gage/Gaige: (French): a pledge or pawn
Galbraith: (Scottish): a foreigner
Gale/Galen: (Gaelic): tranquil; (English): festive party: (Greek): healer, calm
Galileo: (Hebrew): one who comes from Galilee
Gallagher: (Irish & Gaelic): eagle helper
Galt: (English): from the wooded land
Gan: (Chinese): dare, adventure
Gannon: (Irish & Gaelic): fair-skinned
Garcia: (Spanish): one who is brave in battle
Gared: (English): mighty with a spear
Garen/Garin/Garren/Garrin: (English): mighty spearman
Garfield: (English): battlefield
Garnet: (English): gem, armed with a spear; (French): keeper of grain
Garrett: (Irish): to watch
Garrick: (English): oak spear
Garrison: (French): prepared
Garroway: (English): spear fighter
Garry/Gary: (English): mighty spearman
Garson: (English): the son of Gar
Garth: (Scandinavian): keeper of the garden
Gaston: (French): a man from Gastony
Gavin: (English): little hawk; (Welsh): hawk of the battle
Gaylord: (French): merry lord, jailer
Geming: (Chinese): revolution
Gen: (Chinese): root
Gene: (English): a well-born man
Genovese/Geno: (Italian): from Genoa, Italy

Gentry: (English): gentleman
Geoffrey/Geffrey/Jeffrey/Geoff/Geff/Jeff: (English): a man of peace
George: (English): farmer
Gerald/Gerry: (German): one who rules with the spear
Gerard: (French): one who is mighty with the spear
Geronimo: (Greek & Italian): a famous chef
Gervaise: (French): honorable
Gibson: (English): son of Gilbert
Gideon: (Hebrew & Israel): great warrior
Gilbert/Gil: (French): bright promise: (English): trustworthy
Giles: (Greek): resembling a young goat
Gill: (Gaelic): servant
Gilmore: (Irish): devoted to the Virgin Mary
Gilroy: (Irish): devoted to the king
Gino: (Greek): a diminutive form of Eugene, which means well-born man
Giovanni/Gian: (Italian); God is gracious
Guiseppe: (Italian): God will add
Gizmo: (American): playful
Glade: (English): from the clearing in the woods
Glendon: (Scottish): fortress in the glen
Glenn: (Scottish): glen, valley
Glover: (English): one who makes gloves
Goddard: (German): divinely firm
Godfrey: (German): God is peace
Godric: (English): power of God
Goldwin: (English): a golden friend
Goliath: (Hebrew): exiled
Gomer: (Hebrew): completed, finished
Gomez: (Spanish): man
Gonzalo:(Spanish): wolf
Goode: (English): upstanding
Gordon: (Gaelic): from the great hill, hero
Grady: (Gaelic): famous, noble
Graham: (Scottish): from the gray home
Granger: (English): farmer
Grant: (Latin): great
Granville: (French): from the large village
Gray: (English): gray-haired
Grayson: (English): son of the bailiff
Gregory/Greg: (English & Greek): vigilant
Griffin: (Latin): prince, (Welsh): strong in faith
Griffith: (Welsh): mighty chief
Grover: (English): grove
Guang: (Chinese): light
Guido: (Italian): guide
Guillermo: (Spanish): a form of William, which means protector
Gunner/Gunther: (Scandinavian): warrior
Gus: (German): revered
Gustav: (Scandinavian): of the staff of the gods
Guthrie: (German): war hero
Guy: (French): guide; (Hebrew): valley; (Celtic): sensible; (Latin America): living spirit

Hackett/Hackman: (German & French): little wood cutter
Hadley: (English & Irish): from the heath covered meadow
Hagen: (Gaelic): youthful
Haig: (English): enclosed with hedges

Haim: (Hebrew): giver of life
Haines: (English): from the vine-covered cottage
Hakin: (Arabic): wise and intelligent
Hal: (English): ruler of the army
Hallan: (English): dweller at the hall
Halley: (English): from the hall near the meadow
Halliwell: (English): from the holy spring
Halsey: (English): Hal's island
Hamid: (Arabic): praised
Hamilton: (English): from the flat-topped hill
Hamlet: (English): home
Hammond: (English): village
Hancock: (English): one who owns a farm
Hanford: (English): from the high ford
Hank: (Dutch & German): rules his household
Hanley: (English): from the high meadow
Hannibal: (Phoenician): grace of god
Hans: (German & Hebrew): gift from God; (Scandinavian): God is gracious
Hansel: (Hebrew): gift from God; (Scandinavian): God is gracious
Harcourt: (French): fortified dwelling
Harding: (English): brave, manly
Hardwin: (English): brave friend
Harim: (Arabic): superior
Harlan: (English): hare's land
Harley: (English): hare's meadow
Harlow: (English): from the army on the hill
Harold: (Scandinavian): ruler of the army
Harper: (English): one who plays or makes harps
Harrington: (English): from the herring town
Harrison: (English): son of Harry
Harry/Harris: (German): home or house ruler
Hartford: (English): from the stag's ford
Hartley: (English): from the stage meadow
Hartman: (German): hard, strong
Hartwell: (English): deer well
Harvey: (English): strong, ready for battle
Hasam: (Turkish): reaper, harvester
Hasani: Swahili: handsome
Hasim: (Arabic): decisive
Hasin: (Hindu): laughing
Haven: (Dutch): safe harbor or port
Hawk: (English): hawk
Hawkins: (English): resembling a small hawk
Hawthorne: (English): from the hawthorn tree
Hayden: (English & Welsh): in the meadow or valley
Hayes: (English): from the hedged place
He: (Chinese): yellow river
Hea: (Korean): grace
Heath: (English): from the heath wasteland
Heathcliff: (English): cliff near the heath
Heaton: (English): from the town on high ground
Hector: (Greek): steadfast, the prince of Troy
Hedley: (English): heather-filled meadow
Hee: (Korean): brightness
Heinrich: (German): a form of Henry, which means rules his household
Helio: (Greek): god of the sun

Henderson: (Scottish): son of Henry
Heng: (Chinese): eternal
Henley: (English): from the high meadow
Henrik: (German): ruler of the home
Henry: (English, German & French): rules his household
Herbert: (German): glorious soldier
Hercules: (Greek): son of Zeus
Herman: (German): soldier
Hermes: (Greek): stone pile
Hero: (Greek): great defender
Hershel: (Hebrew): resembling a deer
Hewitt: (English): little smart one
Hillard: (German): brave warrior
Hilton: (English): town on a hill
Hiro: (Japanese): widespread
Hiromi: (Japanese): widespread beauty; wide-seeing
Hirum: (Hebrew): noblest, exalted
Hobart: (American): having a shining intellect
Hobson: (English): son of Robert
Hoffman: (German): influential
Hogan: (Irish & Gaelic): young, young at heart
Holbrook: (English): brook in the hollow
Holcomb: (English): from the deep valley
Holden: (English): from a hollow in the valley
Holland: (American): from the Netherlands
Hollis: (English): from the holly tree
Holt: (English): wood, by the forest
Homer: (Greek & English): pledge, promise
Hong: (Chinese): wild swan
Hop: (Chinese): agreeable
Horace/Horatio: (French): hour, time
Horton: (English): garden estate
Houghton: (English): settlement on the headland
Houston: (Gaelic): from Hugh's town: (English): from the town on the hill
Howard: (English): guardian of the home
Howe: (German): high
Howell: (Welsh): remarkable
Hoyt: (Irish): mind, spirit
Hu: (Chinese): tiger
Huan: (Chinese): happiness
Hubert: (German): having a shining intellect
Hud: (Arabic): religion, a Muslim prophet
Hudson: (English): son of the hooded man
Hugh/Hugo: (English): intelligent
Humbert/Humberto: (German): brilliant strength
Humphrey: (German): peaceful strength
Hung: (Vietnamese): brave
Hunter: (English): one who hunts
Huntley: (English): hunter's meadow
Hurley: (Irish): sea tide
Hurst: (Irish): dense grove, thicket
Hussein: (Arabic): little, handsome
Hutton: (English): house on the jutting ledge
Huxley: (English): Hugh's meadow
Huy: (Vietnamese): glorious
Hy: (Vietnamese): hopeful

Hyatt: (English): high gate
Hyde: (English): animal hide
Hyo: (Korean): filial duty
Hyun: (Korean): wisdom

Iago: (Welsh & Spanish): supplanter
Ian: (Scottish): gift from God
Ibsen: (German): archer's son
Ichabod: (Hebrew): the glory has gone
Ignacio: (Italian): fiery
Ignatius/Iggy: (Latin): fiery
Igor: (Scandinavian): hero; (Russian): soldier
Ike: (Hebrew): full of laughter
Iker: (Spanish): visitation
Ilias: (Greek): form of Elijah, which means the Lord is my God
Indiana: (English): from the land of the Indians, the state of Indiana
Ingo: (Scandinavian): lord; (Danish): from the meadow
Ingram: (Scandinavian): a raven of peace
Ioan: (Greek, Bulgarian & Romanian): a form of John, which means God is gracious
Ira: (Hebrew & Israel): watchful
Irv/Irvin/Irving: (Irish): handsome
Irwin: (English): friend of the wild boar
Isaac: (Biblical): he will laugh
Isaiah: (Hebrew): the Lord is generous; (Israel): salvation by God
Isamu: (Japanese): courageous
Isas: (Japanese): meritorious
Isham: (English): from the iron one's estate
Ishmael: (Hebrew, Israel & Spanish): God listens, God will hear
Isidore: (Greek): a gift of Isis
Israel: (Israel): prince of God; (Hebrew): may God prevail
Ivan: (Slavic): God is gracious
Ives: (Scandinavian): the archer's bow
Izod: (Irish): light haired
Jabari: (African): valiant
Jabbar: (Indian): one who consoles others
Jabin: (Hebrew): God has built
Jabo: (American): feisty
Jacinto: (Spanish): resembling a hyacinth
Jack: (English): God is gracious; (Hebrew): supplanter
Jackson: (English): son of Jack; (Scottish): God has been gracious
Jacob: (Biblical): supplanter; (Hebrew): he grasps the heel
Jacobo: (Spanish): supplanter
Jacques: (French): supplanter
Jaden: (American): God has heard
Jafar: (Hindu): little stream
Jagger: (English): a carter, to carry
Jai: (Tai): heart
Jaime/Jamie: (Spanish): supplanter
Jake: (Hebrew): he grasps the heel
Jaleel/Jalen: (American): one who heals others
Jamal/Jamaal/Jamall/Jamaul: (Arabic): handsome
Jamar: (American): handsome
James: (English): supplant, replace; (Israel): supplanter
Jameson/Jamieson: (English): son of James
Jan: (Dutch): a form of John, which means God is gracious
Janus: (Latin American): god of beginnings

Janson/Jansen: (Dutch): son of Jan
Japheth: (Hebrew): handsome
Jared: (Hebrew): descending
Jarek: (Slavic): born in January
Jaron: (Hebrew): he will sing
Jarrett/Jerritt: (English): one who is strong with a spear
Jarvis: (German): skilled with a spear
Jasdeep: (Sikh): the lamp radiating Gods' glories
Jason: (Greek): to heal
Jasper/Jaspar: (Hebrew, French & English): precious stone
Javier/Xavier: (Spanish): owner of a new house
Jax: (American): son of Jack
Jaxon: (American): son of Jack
Jay: (German): swift; (French): blue jay; (English): to rejoice; (Latin America): a crow
Jayce/Jace: (American): God is my salvation
Jayden: (American): God has heard
Jaylen: (English); to rejoice
Jazz: (American): jazz
Jean: (French): a form of John, which means God is gracious
Jeb/Jed/Jebidiah/Jedidiah: (Hebrew): one who is loved by God
Jefferson: (English): son of Jeffrey, which means divine peace
Jeffrey: (French, German & English): divine peace
Jensen: (Scandinavian): God is gracious
Jerald: (English): one who rules with the spear
Jeremiah: (Hebrew): may Jehovah exalt; (Israel): sent by God
Jeremy: (Israel): God will uplift
Jericho: (Arabic): city of the moon
Jermaine: (French): a man from Germany; (Latin): brotherly
Jerome: (Greek): of the sacred name
Jess: (Israel): wealthy
Jesse: (Hebrew): wealthy; (Israel): God exists; (English): Jehovah exists
Jesus: (Hebrew): God is my salvation
Jethro: (Hebrew & Israel): excellence
Jett: (English): resembling the black gemstone
Jiang: (Chinese): fire
Jim: (English): supplanter
Jin: (Chinese): gold
Jiro: (Japanese): second son
Jo: (Japanese): God will increase
Joab: (Israel): paternity, voluntary
Joachim/Joaquin: (Hebrew): God will establish
Job/Jobe: (Hebrew): afflicted
Jock: (Scottish): God is gracious
Jody: (Hebrew): a diminutive form of Joseph, which means God will increase
Joel: (Hebrew): Jehovah is God; (Israel): God is willing
Johann: (German): God's gracious gift
John: (Israel): God is gracious; Jehovah has been gracious
Johnnie: (French, English & Hebrew): diminutive of John, which means God is gracious
Johnson: (Scottish & English): son of John
Jonah: (Hebrew & Israel): a dove
Jonas: (Hebrew): gift from God; (Spanish): dove; (Israel): accomplishing
Jonathan: (Hebrew): Jehovah has given: (Israel): gift of God
Joo: (Korean): jewel
Jordan: (Hebrew): to flow down; (Israel): descendant
Jorell: (American): he saves
Jorge: (Spanish): farmer

Jose: (Spanish): God will add
Joseph/Josef/Jozef: (Biblical): God will increase; (Hebrew): may Jehovah add/give
Joshua: (Hebrew & Biblical): Jehovah saves
Josiah: (Hebrew): Jehovah has healed; (Israel): God has healed
Josue: (Spanish & Hebrew): God is salvation
Journey: (American): one who likes to travel
Jovan: (Latin): majestic
Juan: (Hebrew): gift from God; (Spanish): God is gracious
Juan David: (Spanish): God is gracious/beloved
Juan Diego: (Spanish): God is gracious/Saint James
Juan Esteban: (Spanish): God is gracious/crowned in victory
Juan Felipe: (Spanish): God is gracious/one who loves horses
Juan Ignacio: (Spanish): God is gracious/fiery
Juan Jose: (Spanish): God is gracious/God shall add
Juan Manuel: (Spanish): God is gracious/like God
Juan Pablo: (Spanish): God is gracious/borrowed
Juan Sebastian: (Spanish & Greek): God is gracious/the revered
Judah/Judas/Jude/Judd: (Hebrew & Israel): praised
Jules: (French): youthful, downy-haired
Julian/Julius/Julio: (Spanish, French & Greek): youthful
Jun: (Chinese): truthful; (Japanese): obedient, pure
Jung: (Korean): a righteous man
Justice/Justus: (English): fair and moral
Justin: (English & French): just, true; (Irish): judicious

Kacey: (Irish): vigilant
Kadeem: (Arabic): servant
Kaden/Kade/Kadin/Caden: (Arabic): beloved companion
Kagen: (Irish): fiery
Kai: (American): ocean; (Welsh): keeper of the keys; (Scottish): fire
Kale: (English): manly and strong
Kaleb/Caleb: (Hebrew): resembling an aggressive dog
Kalil/Khalil/Kali: (Arabic): friend
Kamil/Kamal: (Arabic & Hindu): lotus
Kana: (Japanese): powerful
Kane: (Welsh): beautiful; (Gaelic): little warrior
Kang: (Korean): healthy
Kano: (Japanese): powerful
Kareem: (Arabic): noble, distinguished
Karl: (English & Icelandic): man; (French): strong, masculine; (Danish): one who is free
Kavi: (Hindu): poet
Kayden: (American): fighter
Keanu: (Hawaiian): of the mountain breeze
Keaton: (English): from the town of hawks
Kedrick: (English): a form of Cedric, which means battle chieftain
Keefe: (Irish): handsome, loved
Keegan/Kaegan/Keigan: (Gaelic): small and fiery
Keelan/Keilan: (Irish): mighty warrior
Keenan: (Irish): little Keene
Keene: (German): bold, sharp; (English): smart
Keith: (Scottish): wood; (Irish): warrior descending; (Welsh): dwells in the woods
Kellen/Kallen: (Gaelic): slender; (German): from the swamp
Kelley/Kelly: (Celtic): warrior; (Gaelic): one who defends
Kelsey: (English): from the island of ships
Kelvin: (Irish): narrow river
Ken: (Welsh): clear water; (English): royal obligation; (Irish): handsome; (Japanese): strong

Kendall: (English & Celtic): from the bright valley
Kendrick: (English): royal ruler; (Gaelic): champion
Kenley: (English): from the king's meadow
Kennedy: (Scottish): ugly head; (Irish & Gaelic): helmeted
Kenneth: (Celtic, Scottish & Irish): handsome; (English): royal obligation
Kent: (English & Welsh): white; (Celtic): chief
Kenton (English): from the king's town
Kenyon: (Gaelic): blond-haired
Kermit: (Irish): free from envy
Kerrick: (English): king's rule
Kerry: (Irish): dark-haired
Kerwin: (Irish): little, dark
Kesler: (American): energetic and independent
Keung: (Chinese): a universal spirit
Kevin: (Irish & Gaelic): handsome, beautiful; (Celtic): gentle
Khouri: (Arabic): spiritual, a priest
Ki: (Korean): arise
Kidd: (English): resembling a young goat
Kiefer: (German): one who makes barrels
Kieran: (Gaelic): the little dark one
Kiley/Kile: (Gaelic): young; (Irish): young at heart
Kim: (Vietnamese): as precious as gold; (Welsh): leader
Kimball: (Greek): hollow vessel
Kimo: (Hawaiian): a form of James, which means supplant
Kin: (Japanese): golden
Kincaid: (Celtic): the leader during a battle
King: (English): royal ruler
Kingsley: (English): from the king's meadow
Kingston: (English): from the king's village
Kinsey: (English): victorious prince
Kioshi: (Japanese): quiet
Kip/Kipp: (English): from the small pointed hill
Kirby: (Scandinavian): church village
Kirk: (Norse): a man of the church
Kirkland: (English): from the church's land
Kirkley: (English): from the church's meadow
Kit: (English): one who bears Christ inside
Kitoko: (African): handsome
Kiyoshi: (Japanese): quiet one
Knight: (English): noble soldier
Knox: (English): from the hills
Kobe/Kobi/Koby: (African): supplanter; (American): from California
Kode: (English): helpful
Kojo: (African): born on a Monday
Kong: (Chinese): glorious, sky
Kramer: (German): shopkeeper
Kris/Kristian/Kristoff/Kristopher: (Swedish): Christ-bearer
Krishna: (Hindu): delightful, pleasurable
Kuo: (Japanese): approval
Kuro: (Japanese): ninth son
Kurt: (German): brave counselor
Kwame: (Akan): born on a Saturday
Kwan: (Korean): bold character
Kyle: (Gaelic): young; (Irish): young at heart
Kyong: (Korean): brightness
Kyu: (Korean): standard

Lachian: (Gaelic): war-like
Lafayette: (Israel): to God to the mighty
Laine/Lane: (English): narrow road
Laird: (Scottish): lord; (Irish): head of household
Laken: (American): man from the lake
Lamar: (German): famous land; (French): of the sea
Lambert: (Scandinavian): the light of the land
Lamont: (Scandinavian): lawyer
Lance: (German): spear; (French): land
Lancelot: (English & French): servant
Landon: (English): grassy plain; from the long hill
Langley: (English): long meadow
Langston: (English): from the tall man's town
Lanier: (French): one who works with wool
Larkin: (Irish): tough, fierce
Lars/Larry: (Dutch & Latin America): laurels
Larson: (Scandinavian): the son of Lars
LaSalle: (French): from the hall
Lashaun: (American): enthusiastic
Lathan: (American): gift from God
Latimer: (English): an interpreter
Laurent/Laurence: (French & African American): crowned with laurel
Lautaro: (Spanish): crowned with laurel
Lawford: (English): from the ford near the hill
Lawrence/Lawry: (Latin America): crowned with laurel
Lawson: (English): son of Lawrence, which means crowned with laurel
Lazarus/Lazaro: (Hebrew & Israel): God will help
Leander: (Greek): man of lions
Lear: (English): Shakespearean king
Leavitt: (English): a baker
Lee/Leigh: (English): meadow
Legend: (American): memorable
Lei: (Chinese): thunder
Leib: (Yiddish): roaring lion
Leif: (Scandinavian): beloved descendent
Leighton: (English): from the town near the meadow
Leland: (English): meadow land
Len: (Native American): one who plays the flute
Lenard: (French & German): lion, bold
Lenin: (Russian): one who belongs to the river Lena
Lennon: (English): son of love
Lennox: (Scottish): one who owns many elm trees
Leo: (Italian & English): a lion
Leon/Leonard: (Spanish, German, French & Latin America): lion
Leonardo: (German): brave as a lion
Leron: (French): round, circle
Leroy: (French): king
Les/Leslie/Lester: (Scottish): gray fortress
Levi/Levin: (Hebrew & Israel): attached, united as one
Levon: (Armenian): lion
Lew/Lewis: (German): famous warrior
Lewellyn: (Welsh): resembling a lion
Lex/Lexus: (English): a diminutive form of Alexander, which means protector of mankind
Li: (Chinese): having great strength
Liam: (Irish & Gaelic): determined protector

Liang : (Chinese): good man
Lilo: (Hawaiian): generous
Linc/Lincoln: (English): Roman colony at the pool; (Latin America): village
Lindberg: (German): mountain where linden grow
Linden/Lyndon: (English): linden hill
Lindley: (English): from the meadow of linden trees
Linley: (English): flax meadow
Linus: (Latin America): flaxen
Linwood: (English): flax wood
Lionel: (French): lion cub
Liu: (Asian); one who is quiet and peaceful
Livingston: (English): Leif's town
Lloyd: (Celtic, Welsh & English): gray
Locke: (English): forest
Logan: (Irish): small cove; (Scottish): Finnian's servant; (Gaelic): from the hollow
Loki: (Scandinavian): trickster god
Lombard: (Latin): long-bearded
Lon/Lonnie: (Irish): fierce
London: (English): fortress of the moon
Lonzo: (Spanish): ready for battle
Lorcan: (Irish): the small fierce one
Lorenzo: (Italian & Spanish): crowned with laurel
Lot: (Hebrew): hidden covered
Loudon: (German): low valley
Louis: (French): famous warrior
Lovell/Lowell: (French & English): young wolf
Loyal: (English): faithful, loyal
Luc/Luca/Lucian/Lucius: (Latin): surrounded by light
Lucas: (Gaelic, English & Latin America): light
Luciano: (Spanish): light
Lucifer: (Israel): bringing light
Ludwig: (German): famous warrior
Luigi: (Italian): famous warrior
Luis: (Spanish): famous warrior
Luka: (Latin America): light; (Russian): of Luciana
Luke: (Greek & Latin America): light
Luther: (German): soldier of the people
Lux: (Latin): man of the light
Lyle: (French & English): from the island
Lyman: (English): meadow
Lynch: (Irish): mariner
Lyndon: (English): flexible
Lynn: (English): waterfall
Lysander: (Greek): liberator
Mac: (Gaelic): the son of Macarthur or Mackinley
Macallister: (Gaelic): the son of/ Alistair
Macarthur: (Gaelic): the son of Arthur
Macauley: (Scottish): son of righteousness
Macbride: (Scottish): son of a follower of Saint Brigid
Macdonald: (Scottish): son of Donald
Macdougall: (Scottish): son of Dougal
Macintosh: (Gaelic): the son of the thane
Mack/Mac: (Scottish): son
Mackenzie: (Scottish): son of Kenzie
Mackinley: (Gaelic): the son of the white warrior
Maclean: (Irish): son of Leander

Macon: (English): to make
Madden: (Pakistani): well organized
Maddox: (English): son of the Lord; (Celtic): beneficent
Magnus: (Latin): great
Maguire: (Gaelic): the son of the beige one
Mahmud/Mahmoud: (Arabic): one who is praiseworthy
Maitland: (English): from the meadow land
Major: (Latin): greater, military rank
Malachi/Malachy: (Hebrew): angel of God
Malcolm: (Gaelic): follower of St. Columbus
Malik: (African & Arabic): king, master
Malin: (English): strong, warrior
Mallory: (German): army counselor
Malloy: (Irish): noble chief
Manfred: (English): man of peace
Manley: (English): hero's meadow
Mann: (German): man
Manu: (African): the second-born child
Manuel: (Spanish): God is with us
Marcel: (French): little warrior
Marcelo: (Italian & Latin): hammer
Marcos: (Spanish): of mars; (Portuguese): the god of war
Marcus/Marcellus/Marco: (Gaelic): hammer; (Latin America): warlike
Mario: (Hebrew): bitter, king-ruler
Mark/Marc: (Latin): dedicated to Mars, the god of war
Marlon: (French): falcon, of the sea fortress
Marlowe: (English): from the hill by the lake
Marquis: (French): nobleman
Marshall: (French): caretaker of horses; (English): a steward
Marston: (English): from the town near the marsh
Martin: (Latin): dedicated to Mars, the god of war
Marvin: (Welsh): friend of the sea
Mason: (French & English): stone worker
Matias: (Spanish & Hebrew): gift of God
Mathis: (English & Greek): a diminutive form of Matthias, which means gift of God
Matisse: (French): one who is gifted
Matlock: (American): rancher
Matteo: (Italian): gift of God
Matthew: (Hebrew & Biblical): gift of the Lord
Matthias: (English & Greek): gift of God
Maurice: (Latin): dark-skinned
Mauricio: (Spanish): moorish; (Portuguese): dark-skinned
Maverick: (American): independent
Max: (English): greatest
Maximilian: (Latin): greatest
Maximiliano: (Italian): greatest
Maximo (Italian): greatest
Maximus: (Greek): greatest
Maxwell: (English): capable, great spring
Maynard: (English): powerful, brave
McKenna: (Gaelic): the son of Kenna, to ascend; (English): handsome, fiery
McKenzie: (Irish): fair, favored one
McKinley: (English): offspring of the fair hero
Mead: (English): meadow
Mee: (Korean): beauty
Melton/Melville: (English): from the mill town

Melvin: (English): a friend who offers counsel
Mendel: (English): repairman
Mercer: (English): storekeeper
Meredith: (Welsh): guardian from the sea
Merle: (French): blackbird; (English): falcon
Merlin: (Welsh): of the sea fortress
Merrick: (English): ruler of the sea
Merrill: (English): falcon, shining sea
Meyer: (Jewish & Hebrew): shining
Micah: (Israel): like God
Michael: (Biblical & Hebrew): like God
Michelangelo: (Italian): a combination of Michael and Angelo
Mickey: (Irish, English & Hebrew): diminutive of Michael, which means like God
Miguel: (Portuguese & Spanish): who is like God
Mika/Micah: (Finnish): like God; (Japanese): new moon
Mikhail: (Greek & Russian): a form of Michael, which means like God
Miles: (German): merciful; (Latin): a soldier
Milford: (English): from the mill's forge
Miller: (English): one who works at the mill
Milo: (English): soldier
Milton: (English): mill town
Min: (Korean): cleverness
Minh: (Vietnamese): bright
Mitchell: (Hebrew): gift from God
Mohammed/Muhammad: (Arabic): one who is greatly praised
Monroe: (Gaelic): from the red swamp; (Scottish): from the river; (Irish): near the river roe
Montel: (Italian): mountain
Montgomery/Monty/Monte: (French): rich man's mountain
Mooney: (Irish): a wealthy man
Moore: (French): dark-skinned; (Irish & French): surname
Moran: (Irish): a great man
Morell: (French): dark
Morgan: (Celtic): lives by the sea; (Welsh): bright sea
Morley: (English): from the meadow on the moor
Moroccan: (African): one from Morocco
Morris: (Latin America): dark skinned; (English): son of More
Mortimer: (French): of the dead sea
Moses: (Hebrew & Biblical): saved from the water
Muir: (Scottish): moor
Murdoch: (Scottish): from the sea
Murphy: (Gaelic): warrior of the sea
Murray: (Scottish): sailor
Myles: (Latin): soldier
Myron: (Greek): fragrant oil

Nam: (Korean): south
Namir: (Hebrew): leopard
Naoki: (Japanese): honest tree
Naoko: (Japanese): honest
Napier: (French): a mover; (Spanish): new city
Napoleon: (French): fierce one
Narcissus: (Greek): self-love
Naresh: (Indian): king
Nash: (American): adventurer
Nathan/Nathaniel/Nate: (Hebrew & Israel): gift of God
Navarro: (Spanish): from the plains

Naveed: (Persian): our best wishes
Naveen: (Hindu): new; (Irish): beautiful, pleasant
Neal/Neil: (Irish, English & Celtic): a champion
Ned: (English & French): diminutive of Edward, which means wealthy guardian
Nehemiah: (Hebrew): compassion of Jehovah
Nelson: (English, Celtic, Irish & Gaelic): son of Neil
Nemo: (Greek): glen, glade
Neo: (Greek & American): new
Neptune: (Latin): sea ruler
Nero: (Latin & Spanish): stern
Nesbit: (English): nose-shaped bend in a river
Nevada: (Spanish): covered in snow
Neville: (French): from the new village
Nevin: (Irish): worshipper of the saint
Newman: (English): a newcomer
Newton: (English): new town
Ngu/Nguyen: (Vietnamese): sleep
Nicholas/Nico/Nicco: (Greek): victorious people
Nicol: (Scottish & English): victorious
Nicolai: Russian: victorious
Nigel: (English, Gaelic & Irish): champion; (American): ahead
Nikola: (Greek): victorious
Niles: (English): champion
Nino: (Italian): God is gracious; (Spanish): a young boy
Nixon: (English): son of Nick
Noah: (Biblical): rest, peace; (Hebrew): comfort, long-lived
Nobu: (Japanese): faith
Noel: (French): Christmas
Nolan: (Irish & Gaelic): famous; (Celtic): noble
Norbert/Norberto: (Scandinavian): brilliant hero
Norio: (Japanese): man of principles
Norris: (French): northerner
North: (English): from the north
Northcliff: (English): from the northern cliff
Norward: (English): guardian of the north
Noshi: (Native American): fatherly
Nuriel: (Hebrew): God's light
Nye: (English): one who lives on the island

O'Neal/O'Neil: (Irish): Son of Neil
O'Shea/O'Shay: (Irish): son of Shea
Oberon: (German): bear heart
Ocean/Oceanus: (Greek): a titan who rules the sea
Octavio/Octavius: (Latin): eighth
Oden/Odin: (Scandinavian): ruler
Odon: (Hungarian): wealthy protector
Odwin: (German): noble friend
Odysseus: (Greek): wrathful
Ogden: (English): oak valley
Oki: (Japanese): from the center of the ocean
Olaf/Olav/Ole: (Scandinavian): the remaining of the ancestors
Oleg: (Russian): one who is holy
Oliver/Olivier: (French, English, Danish & Latin America): the olive tree; (German): elf army
Olney: (English): from the loner's field
Omar: (Arabian): ultimate devotee; (Hebrew): eloquent speaker
Omega: (Greek): the last great one

Onofrio: (Italian): a defender of peace
Onslow: (Arabic): from the hill of the enthusiast
Oral: (Latin): verbal, speaker
Oram: (English): from the enclosure near the river bank
Ordell: (Latin): of the beginning
Ordway: (Anglo-Saxon): a fighter armed with a spear
Oren: (Hebrew): from the pine tree; (Gaelic): fair-skinned
Orion: (Greek): a hunter in Greek mythology
Orland: (English): from the pointed hill; (Spanish & German): renowned in the land
Orlando: (Spanish): land of gold: (German): famous throughout the land
Orly: (Hebrew): surrounded by light
Ormond: (English): one who defends with a spear
Orpheus: (Greek): an excellent musician
Orrin: (English): river
Orson: (Latin): resembling a bear
Orton: (English): from the settlement by the shore
Orville: (French): golden city; (English): spear-strength
Orwell: (Welsh): of the horizon
Osborn/Osbourne: (Norse): a bear of God
Oscar: (English): a spear of the gods; (Gaelic): a friend of deer
Oswald: (English): the power of God
Oswin: (English): a friend of God
Othello: (Spanish): rich
Otis: (German & Greek): wealthy
Otto: (German): wealthy or prosperous
Ovid: (Latin): a shepherd, egg
Owen: (English, Welsh & Celtic); young warrior; (Irish): born to nobility
Oz: (Hebrew): having great strength
Ozzy: (English): divine ruler

Pablo: (Spanish): a form of Paul, which means small
Pace: (English): a peaceful man
Paco: (Spanish): a man from France
Page/Paige: (French): youthful assistant
Paine/Payne: (Latin): a peasant
Palmer: (English): a pilgrim bearing a palm branch
Pan: (Greek): god of flocks
Pancho: (Spanish): diminutive form of Francisco, which means free
Panya: (African): resembling a mouse
Panyin: (African): the first-born twin
Paolo: (Italian): a form of Paul, which means small
Paris: (Greek): downfall; (French): the capital city of France
Park: (Chinese): the cypress tree
Parker: (English): keeper of the park or forest
Parnell: (French): little Peter
Parry: (Welsh): the son of Harry
Pascal: (French): born at Easter
Patricio: (Spanish): patrician, noble
Patrick: (Latin): a nobleman
Patton: (English): from the town of warriors
Paul: (English & French): small, apostle in the Bible
Pax: (English): peaceful
Paxton: (English): from the peaceful farm; (Latin America): town of peace
Pearce/Pierce: (English): a form of Peter, which means small rock
Pearson: (English): son of Peter
Pedro: (Spanish): solid and strong as a rock

Peeta/Peetamber: (Indian): yellow silk cloth
Pegasus: (Greek): winged horse
Peli: (Latin): happy
Pell: (English): a clerk
Pelton: (English): from the town by the lake
Pembroke: (Welsh): headland
Penley: (English): from the enclosed meadow
Penn: (Latin): pen, quill
Pepe: (Spanish): a diminutive form of Jose, which means God will add
Pepin: (German): determined
Percival: (French): one who can pierce the vale
Percy: (English): piercing the valley
Perez: (Hebrew): to break through
Perry: (English): a familiar form of Peter, which means a small stone or rock
Peter: (Greek & English): a small stone or rock, apostle in the Bible
Peterson: (English): son of Peter
Peyton: (English): from the village of warriors
Pharell/Pharrell: (American): of proven courage
Philip: (French, Greek & English): lover of horses
Phinean/Finian: (Irish): light-skinned, white
Phineas/ Phinneaus/Fineas: (Hebrew): oracle; (Israel): loudmouth; (Egyptian): dark-skinned
Phong: (Vietnamese): of the wind
Pierce: (English): rock
Pierre: (French): a rock
Ping: (Chinese): stable
Placido: (Spanish): serene
Plato: (Greek): broad-shouldered
Platt: (French): flatland
Pollock: (Greek): crown; (English): little rock
Pollux: (Latin American): brother of Helen
Polo: (Tibetan): brave warrior
Ponce: (Spanish): fifth
Porter: (French): gate keeper; (Latin America): door guard
Powell: (English): alert
Prentice: (English): a student
Prescott: (English): from the priest's cottage
Presley: (English): priest's land
Preston: (English): from the priest's farm
Prewitt: (French): brave little one
Primo: (Italian): first, premier quality
Prince: (Latin): chief, prince
Pryor: (Latin): head of the monastery
Puck: (English): elf
Pullman: (English): one who works on a train
Purnam: (English): dweller by the pond
Purvis: (French & English): providing food

Qiang: (Chinese): strong
Qiu: (Chinese): autumn
Quade: (Latin): fourth
Quiad: (Irish): the commander of the army
Quain: (French): clever
Quashawn: (American): tenacious
Quentin: (Latin): fifth
Quigley: (Irish): maternal side
Quillan: (Gaelic): resembling a cub

Quimby: (Scandinavian): woman's estate
Quincy: (English): fifth-born child; (French): estate belonging to Quintus
Quinlan: (Gaelic): strong and healthy man
Quinn: (Celtic): queenly; (Gaelic): one who provides counsel
Quinton/Quinten/Quintin: (Latin): from the queen's town

Radcliff/Radcliffe: (English): red cliff
Rafael/Raphael: (Spanish): one who is healed by God
Rafe: (Irish): a tough man
Rafferty: (Irish): prosperous
Raiden: (Japanese): god of thunder and lightning
Rain/Raine: (American): blessings from above; (Latin): ruler; (English): lord, wise
Rainer: (German): counsel
Raj/Rajan/Rajah: (Hindu): king
Raleigh/Rawley: (English): deer meadow
Ralph: (English): wolf counsel
Ram: (Hindu): god, god-like
Ramon: (Spanish): a wise or mighty protector
Ramsey: (Scottish): island of ravens
Rand/Randy/Randall/Randolph: (German): the wolf shield
Raoul: (French): wolf counsel
Rashad: (Arabic): wise counselor
Raul: (French): a form of Ralph, which means wolf counsel
Ravi: (Hindu): from the sun
Ray: (French): regal; (Scottish): grace; (English): wise protector
Rayburn: (English): deer brook
Raymond: (German): wise protector
Razi: (Aramaic): my secret
Rebel: (American): outlaw
Redford: (English): over the red river, from the reedy ford
Redmond: (German): protecting counselor
Reece/Reese: (English & Welsh): ardent, fiery, enthusiastic
Reed/Reid: (English & French): red-haired
Reeve: (English): a bailiff
Regan/Reagan: (Gaelic): born into royalty
Reginald/Reggie: (Latin): the king's advisor
Regis: (Latin): regal; (Latin America): rules
Reilly: (Gaelic): outgoing
Reinhart/Reynard/Reynold/Renaldo/Rey: (French): wise, bold, courageous
Remi/Remy: (French): oarsman or rower, from Rheims
Remington: (English): from the town of the raven's family
Rene/Renee: (French): reborn
Reuben/Ruben: (Hebrew): behold, a son
Rex: (Latin): king
Rhett: (English): stream
Rhodes: (Greek): where roses grow
Rhys: (Welsh): enthusiasm for life
Ricardo: (Spanish): strong and powerful ruler
Richard: (English, French & German): a strong and powerful ruler
Rico: (German): glory; (Spanish & Cuban): strong ruler
Ridge: (English): from the ridge
Ridley: (English): from the red meadow
Rigby: (English): ruler's valley
Riley: (English): from the rye clearing; (Irish): a small stream
Ringo: (Japanese): peace be with you
Rio: (Spanish & Portuguese): river

Ripley: (English): from the noisy meadow
Rishi: (Hindu): sage
River: (Latin & French): stream, water
Roan: (English): from the Rowan tree
Roark: (Gaelic): champion
Robert: (English, French, German & Scottish): famed, bright, shining
Robin: (English): a diminutive form of Robert, which means famed, bright, shining
Robinson: (English): son of Robin
Rocco: (Italian & German) rest
Rocket/Rockett/Rockitt: (English): fast
Rockford: (English): from the rocky ford
Rockwell: (English): rocky spring
Roden: (English): red valley
Roderick: (German): famous ruler
Rodney: (English): land near the water, island of reeds
Rodrigo: (Spanish): famous ruler
Roger: (German): renowned spearman
Roland/Rollo/Rolle: (French, German & English): renowned in the land
Rolf: (German): wolf counsel
Roman: (Spanish & Latin America): from Rome
Romeo: (Italian, Spanish, Latin America & African American): from Rome
Romulus: (Latin): citizen of Rome
Ronald: (English, Gaelic & Scottish): rules with counsel
Ronan: (Gaelic): resembling a little seal
Ronin: (Japanese): samurai without a master
Rooney: (Gaelic): red-haired
Roosevelt: (Danish): from the field of roses
Rory: (Irish): famous brilliance, famous ruler; (Gaelic): red-haired
Roscoe: (Norwegian): deer forest
Ross: (Scottish): from the peninsula
Roswell: (English): fascinating
Rowan: (Irish): red-haired; (English & Gaelic): from the rowan tree
Roy: (Irish & French): king, regal; (Scottish, Gaelic & Scottish): red, red-haired
Royce: (English): royal, son of the king: (German): famous
Rudolph: (German): a famous wolf
Rufus: (Latin America): redhead
Ruiz: (Spanish): a good friend
Rupert: (German): bright fame
Russell/Russ/Rush: (French): a little red-haired boy
Rusty: (English): one who has red hair or a ruddy complexion
Rutherford: (English): from the cattle's ford
Ryan: (Gaelic): little king; (Irish): kindly, young royalty
Ryder: (English): knight
Ryker: (Danish): a powerful ruler
Rylan/Ryland: (English): the place where rye is grown

Saber: (French): man of the sword
Sacha: (French): protector of mankind
Said/Sa'id/Sayed: (Arabic): happy
Saige/Sage: (English & French): wise one; (English): from the spice
Sailor: (American): sailor
Salem: (Hebrew): peace
Salisbury: (English): fort at the willow pool
Salmon: (Czech): a form of Solomon, which means peaceful
Salvador/Salvatore: (Spanish & Italian): savior
Samson/Sampson: (Hebrew & Israel): bright as the sun

Samuel: (Israel): God hears; (Hebrew): name of God
Sanborn: (English): sandy brook
Sandburg: (English): from the sandy village
Sandeep: (Punjabi): enlightened
Sanford: (English): from the sandy crossing
Sanjay: (American): a combination of Sanford and Jay
Santana: (Spanish): saintly
Santiago: (Spanish): named for Saint James
Santino: (Italian): little angel
Santo: (Italian): a holy man
Sargent: (French): army officer
Satchel: (French): Saturn
Saturn: (Latin): the god of agriculture
Saul: (Israel): borrowed: (Hebrew & Spanish): asked for
Sawyer: (English): one who works with wood
Saxon/Sax: (English): a swordsman
Sayid: (African): lord and master
Schaffer/Schaeffer: (German): a steward
Schuman: (German): shoemaker
Scott: (Scottish): wanderer
Scout: (French): scout
Scully: (Irish): herald; (Gaelic): town crier
Seaman: (English): a mariner
Seamus: (Irish): a form of James, which means supplant
Sean/Shawn: (Irish): God is gracious
Sebastian: (Greek): the revered one
Sergio/Sergei/Serge: (Latin, Italian & Russian): a servant
Seth: (Hebrew): anointed; (Israel): appointed
Seton/Seaton: (English): from the farm by the sea
Seung: (Korean): a victorious successor
Seven: (American): the number seven
Sexton: (English): church custodian
Seymour: (French): from the town of Saint Maur
Shade: (English): secretive
Shan: (Chinese): mountain
Shane: (Hebrew): gift from God; (Irish): God is gracious
Shannon: (Gaelic): having ancient wisdom
Sharif: (Arabic): noble
Shaw: (English): from the woodland
Shawn: (Irish): a form of Sean, which means God is gracious
Shea: (Irish): majestic, fairy place
Sheffield: (English): from the crooked field
Sheldon: (English): from the steep valley
Shelton: (English): from the farm on the ledge
Shen: (Chinese): deep spiritual thought
Shepherd: (English): one who herds sheep
Sheridan: (Irish, English & Celtic): untamed; (Gaelic): bright, a seeker
Sherlock: (English): fair-haired
Sherman: (English): one who cuts wool cloth
Sherwin: (English): swift runner
Shiloh: (Hebrew): he who was sent, God's gift, the one to whom it belongs; (Israel): peaceful
Shin: (Japanese): truth
Shiro: (Japanese): fourth-born son
Sidney: (English): wide island
Siddhartha: (Hindu): the original name of Buddha
Siegfried: (German): victorious peace

Sierra: (Spanish): from the jagged mountain range
Sigmund: (German): victorious protector
Silas: (Latin America): man of the forest
Silver: (English): precious metal, the color silver
Simba: (African): lion
Simmons: (Hebrew): the son of Simon
Simon: (Israel): it is heard
Simpson: (Hebrew): son of Simon
Sinclair: (English): man from Saint Clair
Singh: (Hindu): lion
Skelly: (Irish): storyteller
Skylar/Schuyler: (Dutch): sheltering
Slade: (English): child of the valley
Slater: (English): one who works with slate
Sloan: (English): raid; (Irish, Celtic, Scottish & Gaelic): fighter, warrior
Smith: (English): artisan, tradesman
Socrates: (Greek): wise, learning
Solomon: (Hebrew & Israel): peaceful
Soo: (Korean): excellent, long life
Spalding: (English): divided field
Speck: (German): bacon
Spence/Spencer: (English): dispenser, provider
Stanford: (English): from the stony ford
Stanley: (English): stony meadow
Stanton: (English): from the stony ford
Stavros: (Greek): one who is crowned
Steadman: (English): one who lives at the farm
Stefan: (German, Polish & Swedish): a form of Steven, which means crowned one
Stefano/Stephano: (Italian): a form of Steven, which means crowned one
Stephen/Steven: (English & Greek): crowned one
Sterling: (English): valuable
Stern: (English): austere
Stone/Stony: (English): stone
Storm/Stormy: (English): tempest; (American): impetuous nature
Striker: (American): aggressive
Stuart: (Scottish): steward; (English): bailiff; (Irish): keeper of the estate
Sullivan: (Gaelic): dark eyes
Sully: (English): from the southern meadow
Sven: (Scandinavian): youth
Sydney: (English): wide island
Sylvester/Sly: (Latin): man from the forest

Taft: (French): from the homestead
Taggart: (Gaelic): son of a priest
Tai: (Chinese): large; (Vietnamese): prosperous, talented
Taj: (Indian): one who is crowned
Tam: (Vietnamese): having heart, the number eight
Tama: (Japanese): jewel
Tanner: (English & German): leather worker
Tannon: (German): from the fir tree
Tao: (Chinese): one who has a long life
Tarek/Tarik/Tariq: (Arabic): conqueror
Tate/Tatum: (English): cheerful
Taurean: (Latin): strong
Tavor/Tavarus/Tavaris: (Aramaic): misfortune
Taye: (Ethiopian): *one who has been seen*

Taylor: (English & French): a tailor
Teagan: (Gaelic): handsome, attractive
Ted/Teddy: (English): a gift from God
Teller/Telly: (English & Greek): storyteller
Tennessee: (Native American): from the state of Tennessee
Tennyson: (English): a form of Dennison, which means son of Dennis
Terrell: (German): thunder ruler
Terrence/Terrance: (Latin America): tender, gracious
Tex: (English): of Texas
Texas: (Native American): one of many friends, from the state of Texas
Thaddeus: (Hebrew): valiant, wise: (Greek): praise, one who has courage
Thang: (Vietnamese): victorious
Thanh: (Vietnamese): finished
Thatcher: (English): one who repairs roofs
Theodore: (Greek): divine gift
Thiago: (Spanish, Portuguese & Brazilian): Saint James
Thierry: (French): a dorm of Theodore, which means divine gift
Thomas: (Hebrew, Greek & Dutch): twin
Thor: (Norse): god of thunder
Thorne: (English): from the thorn bush
Thurmond: (English): defended by Thor
Thurston: (English): Thor's town
Tien: (Chinese): heaven
Tiernan: (Gaelic): lord of the manor
Tiger: (English): powerful cat
Tilden: (English): tilled valley
Tilford: (English): prosperous ford
Timon: (Hebrew): honor
Timothy: (Greek & English): to honor God
Tito: (Italian): honor
Titus: (Greek): of the giants; (Latin): great defender
Tobias: (Hebrew & Israel): God is good
Toby: (English): God is good
Todd: (Scottish): fox
Tolbert: (English): tax collector
Tomas: (German): a form of Thomas, which means twin
Tong: (Vietnamese): fragrant
Torin: (Irish): chief
Torrence: (Irish): knolls
Travis: (French): to cross over
Trent: (Welsh): dwells near the rapid stream
Trenton: (English): town of Trent
Trevor: (Welsh): from the large village
Trey/Treat: (English & Latin): third-born child
Treyvon: (American): a form of Trevon, which is a combination of Trey and Von
Trigg: (Norse): truthful
Tripp: (English): traveler
Tristan: (English, Celtic & French): outcry, tumult; (Welsh): noisy; (Irish): bold
Trong: (Vietnamese): respected
Troy: (French): curly haired; (Irish): foot soldier
True: (English): loyal
Twain: (English): divided in two
Tybalt: (Latin): he who sees the truth
Tye/Ty: (English): from the fenced-in pasture
Tyler: (English): maker of tiles
Tyr: (Norway): god of war

Tyrell: (American & English): thunder ruler
Tyrone/Tyronne: (French): from Owen's land
Tyson: (French): explosive; (English): son of Tye

Udell: (English): from the valley of yew trees
Udi: (Hebrew): one who carries a torch
Ugo: (Italian): a great thinker
Ulmer: (German): having the fame of a wolf
Ulrich: (German): wolf ruler
Ulysses: (Latin): hateful
Unique: (Latin): only one; (American): unlike others
Unity: (English): unity, togetherness
Upton: (English): upper town
Uranus: (Greek): mythical father of the titans
Urban: (Latin): city dweller, courteous
Uri: (Hebrew): God is my light
Usher: (Latin): from the mouth of the river; (English): doorkeeper
Utah: (Native American): people of the mountains, the state of Utah
Uzi: (Hebrew): having great power
Uziel: (Hebrew): God is my strength

Vadim: (Russian): god looking
Valentine/Val: (Latin): strong and healthy
Valentino: (Italian): brave or strong; (Latin America): health or love
Vance: (English): windmill dweller
Vandyke: (Danish): from the dike
Vardon: (French): from the green hill
Varick: (German): a protective ruler
Vaughn: (Celtic): small
Vernon/Vern: (Latin): youthful, young at heart; (French & English): alder tree grove
Verrill: (German): masculine; (French): loyal
Vicente: (Spanish): a form of Vincent, which means winner
Victor: (Spanish & Latin America): winner
Vijay: (Hindu): victorious
Vikram: (Hindu): valorous
Vincent: (English & Latin America): conquering, victorious
Vicente: (Spanish): conquering, victorious
Vinson: (English): son of Vincent
Virgil/Vergil: (English): flourishing; (Latin America): strong
Vito: (Latin): one who gives life
Vladimir: (Slavic): a famous prince
Vulcan: (Latin): the god of fire

Wade: (English): ford, cross the river
Wadley: (English): from the meadow near the ford
Wadsworth: (English): from the estate near the ford
Wagner: (German): wagoner
Wainwright: (English): one who builds wagons
Waite: (English): watchman
Walden: (English): wooded valley
Walker: (English): one who trods the cloth
Wallace: (Scottish): a man from the south
Walter: (German): the commander of the army
Walton: (English): walled town
Wane/Wayne: (English): craftsman, wagon maker
Wang: (Chinese): hope, wish

Warden: (English): guard
Wardell: (English): from the guardian's hill
Warner/Werner: (German & English): defender
Warren: (English): to preserve; (German): protector, loyal
Warrick: (English): a protective ruler
Washington: (English): town near water
Watson: (English): the son of Walter
Waverly: (English): quaking aspen
Wayan: (Indonesian): first son
Waylon: (English): land by the road
Wayne/Wane: (English): craftsman, wagon maker
Webb: (English): weaver
Webster: (English): a weaver
Wei: (Chinese): a brilliant man, great strength
Weiss: (German): white
Welborne: (English): spring-fed stream
Wendall/Wendell: (German): a wanderer
Wentworth: (English): village, from the white one's estate
Wesley: (English & German): from the west meadow
West: (English): from the west
Weston: (English): west town
Wheatley: (English): wheat field
Whit: (English): white-skinned
Whitby: (English): from the white farm
Whitfield: (English): from the white field
Whitley/Whit: (English): from the white meadow
Whitman: (English): white-haired
Whitmore: (English): white moor
Whitney: (English): white island
Wickley: (English): village meadow
Wilbur: (English): bright willows, fortification
Wilder: (English): wilderness
Wiley: (English): crafty
Wilford: (English): from the willow ford
Wilfred: (German): determined peacemaker
William/Willem: (English, German & French): protector
Willis: (English): son of Willie, which is a diminutive form of William
Wilmer: (German): determined and famous
Wilson: (English & German): son of William
Windsor: (English): riverbank with a winch
Winston: (English): joy stone
Winter: (American): the season
Winthrop: (English): from the friendly village
Winton: (English): from the enclosed pastureland
Wolf: (English): the animal, wolf
Wolfgang: (German): wolf quarrel
Woodley: (English): wooded meadow
Woodrow: (English): forester, row of houses
Wyatt: (English): guide, wide, wood, famous bearer; (French): son of the forest guide
Wyndham: (English): from the windy village

Xander: (Greek): a diminutive form of Alexander, which means protector of mankind
Xannon: (American): from an ancient family
Xavier: (Basque): owner of a new house; (Arabic): one who is bright
Xiu: (Chinese): cultivated
Xoan: (Gaelic): God is gracious

Xue: (Chinese): studious

Yale: (Welsh): from the fertile upland
Yan/Yann: (Russian): a form of John, which means God is gracious
Yancy: (Native American): Englishman
Yang: (Chinese): people of goat tongue
Yao: (Ewe): born on a Tuesday
Yaphet: (Hebrew): handsome
Yardley: (English): from the fenced-in meadow
Yasir: (Arabic): well-off financially
Yeo: (Korean): mildness
Yeoman: (English): a man-servant
Yitzchak: (Hebrew): a form of Isaac, which means he will laugh
Yo: (Cambodian): honest
Yohan: (German): God is gracious
Yong: (Korean): courageous
York: (Celtic, English & Latin America): from the yew tree
Yosef: (Hebrew): a form of Joseph, which means God will increase
Yoshi: (Japanese): adopted son
You: (Chinese): friend
Young: (Korean): forever, unchanging
Yul/Yule: (English): born at Christmas
Yuri: (Russian & Ukrainian): a form of George, which means farmer
Yves: (French): a young archer

Zachariah/Zacarias/Zachary: (Hebrew): Jehovah has remembered; (Israel): remembered by the Lord
Zaden/Zayden: (Arabic & Dutch): a sower of seeds
Zale: (Greek): having the strength of the sea
Zander: (Slavic): helper and defender of mankind
Zane/Zain: (Hebrew): gift from God; (Arabian): beloved
Zared: (Hebrew): one who is trapped
Zarek: (Polish): may God protect the king
Zavier: (Arabic): a form of Xavier, which means bright
Zebulun/Zebulon/Zeb: (Hebrew & Israel): habitation
Zedekiah/Zed: (Hebrew): God is mighty and just
Zeke: (English): strengthened by God
Zeno: (Greek): cart, harness
Zephyr: (Greek): west wind
Zeus: (Greek): powerful one
Zhen: (Chinese): astonished
Zia: (Hebrew): trembling
Zian: (Chinese): peace
Zigfrid/Ziggy: (Latvian & Russian): a form of Siegfried, which means victorious peace
Zion: (Hebrew): from the citadel
Zoltan: (Hungarian): kingly

www.ingramcontent.com/pod-product-compliance
Lightning Source LLC
LaVergne TN
LVHW081354060426
835510LV00013B/1819